D1282459

# Executive Behaviour

*This is a volume in the*
*Arno Press collection*

# HISTORY OF MANAGEMENT THOUGHT

**Advisory Editors**
Kenneth E. Carpenter
Alfred D. Chandler

**Consulting Editor**
Stuart Bruchey

*See last pages of this volume*
*for a complete list of titles*

# Executive Behaviour

SUNE CARLSON

## ARNO PRESS
A New York Times Company
New York • 1979

WILLIAM MADISON RANDALL LIBRARY UNC AT WILMINGTON

Editorial Supervision: BRIAN QUINN
Reprint Edition 1979 by Arno Press Inc.

Reprinted from a copy in the Library of the University
of Illinois

HISTORY OF MANAGEMENT THOUGHT
  AND PRACTICE
ISBN for complete set: 0-405-12306-X
See last pages of this volume for titles.

Manufactured in the United States of America

————

**Library of Congress Cataloging in Publication Data**

Carlson, Sune, 1909-
   Executive behaviour.

   (History of management thought)
   Reprint of the ed. published by Stromberg, Stockholm.
   Includes bibliographical references and index.
   1. Executives.  2.  Industrial management.
3.  Executives--Sweden.  4.  Industrial management--
Sweden.  I.  Title.  II.  Series.
HF5500.2.C38  1979          658.4'009485        79-7535
ISBN 0-405-12317-5

HF5500
.2
.C38
1979

# Executive Behaviour

209509

*By the same author*

A STUDY ON THE PURE THEORY OF PRODUCTION

BUSINESS STATISTICS
*(in Swedish, Second Impression)*

BUSINESS MANAGEMENT AND BUSINESS LEADERS
*(in Swedish, Second Impression)*

A SWEDISH CASE STUDY ON PERSONNEL RELATIONS
*(with Per Ernmark)*

# Executive Behaviour

A Study of the Work Load and the
Working Methods of Managing Directors

BY

SUNE CARLSON

*Professor of Business Administration in the
Stockholm School of Economics*

STRÖMBERGS 5 STOCKHOLM

Copyright 1951 by

C. A. STRÖMBERG AKTIEBOLAG, PUBL.

Valhallavägen 184, Stockholm


*All rights reserved. No part of this book may be reproduced in any form,
by mimeograph or any other means without permission in writing by the
publisher.*

Printed in Sweden by

UDDEVALLA

BOHUSLÄNINGENS AB

1951

TO

THE MANAGING DIRECTORS WHO
COURAGEOUSLY AND GRACIOUSLY
HAVE PLAYED THE RÔLE OF GUINEA-
PIGS IN THIS STUDY

# CONTENTS

[7]

# LIST OF FIGURES

# PREFACE

In her book *Sex and Temperament in Three Primitive Societies* Margaret Mead tells us about a mountain people, the Arapesh, who are characterized by their friendliness, their sociability and their readiness to help each other. When describing the leaders of this people she says: "No one, it is assumed, really wants to be a leader, a 'big man'. 'Big men' have to plan, have to initiate exchanges, have to strut and swagger and talk in loud voices, have to boast of what they have done in the past and are going to do in the future. All of this the Arapesh regard as most uncongenial, difficult behaviour, the kind of behaviour in which no normal man would indulge if he could possibly avoid it. It is a rôle that the society forces upon a few men in certain recognized ways." Even a hasty study of the behaviour of chief executives in Swedish firms indicates that there are both similarities and differences between 'big men' in Swedish industry and 'big men' among the Arapesh.

But the reader must not be misled into thinking that this is an anthropological study of sex and temperament of managing directors. It is something much less fascinating and spectacular; it is merely an attempt to study the behaviour of the directors in their daily work. Nevertheless, in the course of this work I have often felt as I believe a social anthropologist must feel when he has to study the big chiefs of an unknown tribe. I have seen many strange things and generally I have lacked the necessary hypotheses to arrange my observations in a neat theoretical system. I have often felt lost and bewildered. But if one is completely lost, it is not a bad plan, says Barbara Wootton, to try to make a note of nearly everything that one can see. "After a time, something that makes sense may emerge from some region of what till then looked like complete confusion." This is exactly what i have done, and the ideas that have emerged I have put into this book. I sincerely hope that they make some sense, or that if they do not, they will at least stimulate discussion and in that way be fruitful for further research.

The purpose of this study has been neither to develop any normative rules as to how executives should behave, nor to describe their "typical" or "average" behaviour. But by studying a series of individual cases I have hoped to find certain common behaviour patterns and some general relationships which characterize these patterns. Thus far I have travelled only a short distance towards this goal. Although until now the results of my study have taken the form of general ideas rather than of clearly stated hypotheses, I have wanted to make them available even at this early stage. Scientific research is mainly a way of acquiring knowledge for the student who does it, and in so far as one student is able to help others by reporting his failures and successes I think he should do.

The first two chapters of this book have been published in part as separate articles. The first pages of Chapter 1 are taken from a report published in the proceedings of *The Eighth International Management Congress Stockholm 1947,* and other portions of that and the following chapter have been publiched in *British Management Review.*

In the three years that this study has been in progress I have received so much help, criticism and encouragement that I cannot possibly acknowledge it all. But there are some things that I want to mention specially. First of all, I am of course greatly indebted to the members of the Administrative Problems Study Group and the International Association of Department Stores who have not only volunteered as research objects in this study, but have cooperated in all possible ways to make the study a success. My sincere thanks are also due to my assistant Mr. Rune Höglund who has been my faithful helper and adviser from the time when the first plans of the study were drawn up until the last proof was sent to the printer. Finally I want to use this opportunity to thank the members of the Faculty of Economics and Social Studies at the University of Manchester, whose generous aid in the form of a Simon Research Fellowship during the Summer Term 1950 greatly facilitated the writing of this book.

The Stockholm School of Economics
November, 1950

*Sune Carlson*

# Chapter 1

# THE SETTING OF THE PROBLEM

L'homme est naturellement métaphysicien et orgueilleux; il a pu croire que les créations idéales de son esprit qui correspondent à ses sentiments représentaient aussi la réalité. D'où il suit que la méthode expérimentale n'est point primitive et naturelle à l'homme, et que ce n'est qu'après avoir erré longtemps dans les discussions théologiques et scolastiques qu'il a fini par reconnaître la stérilité de ses efforts dans cette voie.

*Claude Bernard*

## 1. THE ORIGIN OF THE STUDY

In the spring of 1944 a group of Swedish business executives met to discuss the general problem of executive education. The outcome of this discussion was the formation of an informal organization devoted exclusively to research and discussion of top-management questions. The organization was called "The Administrative Problems Study Group". From its start it has worked in close contact with the Department of Business Administration at the Stockholm School of Economics, and I have myself served as its director of research. The group still exists, and it has at present as ordinary members the managing directors of 12 leading Swedish business firms. In principle these firms should be non-competing, so that the members feel absolutely free to express their opinions. Actually there are two banks and two insurance companies represented in the group. Other branches represented are:

[13]

the mining and metal refining industry,
the coal mining and pottery industry,
the iron and steel industry,
the mechanical engineering industry,
the textile industry,
the printing industry,
the brewing industry, and
the department store trade.

The members of the group meet regularly 2 to 4 times a year for a full day's discussion of a selected administrative problem. It is the function of the research director to plan these discussions and to collect, analyze and present all the necessary material. As soon as a problem for the next discussion has been selected, the director and his assistant start to collect all pertinent information that can be obtained from the literature in the field. A detailed questionnaire is drawn up and sent out to the members, who are asked to report everything they have done or planned to do with respect to the problem at hand, a task which often requires extensive investigation. While this work is going on, the firms are usually visited by the research director, who, even at this preliminary stage, can ask questions and get information on different points which otherwise might be overlooked. In some cases the members prepare a copy of their report or some other material of interest for all the other members, while in other cases they send in one copy only for the research director's use. It is always the task of the director to summarize the findings in a general report, which, together with other material available, is sent out to the members before the group meets. The director also has to prepare a detailed plan and time table for the coming discussion.

When the members finally meet, everyone is well prepared for an interesting discussion. Since the group is small and homogeneous and all the members know each other well, it is possible to be absolutely frank. If a member wants to bring another representative from his firm along to a meeting, or if he wants to send a deputy, this person must be carefully selected in order that he will not hamper the free interchange of ideas. As a whole the group has been very successful in this respect. The stenographic records of a day's discussion often contain more than 200 individual speeches, questions and answers. A summarized report of these records concludes the documents prepared on the particular question dealt with.

The subjects discussed up to the spring of 1947 were:

formal organization of the firm,

company policy with regard to keeping employees informed,

company policy with regard to working conditions, training, health and other personnel services, and

salary administration and promotion policy.

There was some doubt at first whether companies of such different characters as banks, department stores and coal mines would have enough problems in common for a fruitful interchange of experience. The past years have shown that at the company-wide level, most administrative problems are very much the same, irrespective of branch or type of trade. If there is a certain heterogeneousness among the members, this is due not so much to the different branches as to the fact that some companies are located in large cities and others out in the country.

During the last two or three years the group's research activity has been devoted solely to a study of the managing directors' own work. The purpose of this study was never formulated in an exact way, but I think it can be summarized as follows. The studies already made by the group had shown that there were many things that the members could learn both from each other and from the contact with the scientific thinking in the field. The mere fact that each individual member was compelled to re-examine and state his own problems on paper had not been least important. There was no reason why a similar re-examination and interchange of ideas regarding the members' own work would not be just as valuable. There were also other reasons for a study. At present there is a definite demand in Swedish industry for better selection and training procedures at the top-executive level, but in order to satisfy this demand we must know more about how executive work is actually carried out than we do at present. It was also hoped that the study might throw some light on the important problem of public relations. The relationship between the firm and the community at large has changed rapidly during and after the war, and a special study of these changes is also on the group's programme.

While this study was going on in Sweden I was asked to become scientific adviser to a specially appointed "top-management commission" in the International Association of Department Stores.[1] The association has as members eight of the largest department stores in Scandinavia and Western Europe, one in each of eight countries. As a member of this commission I had the opportunity to discuss my Swedish study with the other members, who all were experts on various administrative problems, and I was asked to make a study of the same kind as those I was doing in Sweden on the two chief executives of "Au Printemps" in Paris. The experiences from this latter study have been of special value. While the Swedish study was made in firms with which I have been connected for several years, and of which the organizational structure, the personal set-up and the

---

[1] Cf. H. Pasdermadjian, *Management Research in Retailing*, London 1950, pp. 49—50.

general business policies were familiar to me, I knew very little about "Au Printemps". Thus, I had a chance to apply my investigation technique on new material and in an environment which was quite different from what I was used to.

## 2. THE OBSERVATIONAL APPROACH

"Research reports of social scientists", writes Lloyd Warner in his introduction to the Yankee City Studies, "usually present no more than brief summaries of their methods and even less of the theoretical assumptions and postulates which governed (1) the selection of their specific field of investigation, (2) the choice of facts collected, and (3) the ordering and classification of data during analysis and synthesis. Most reports tend to emphasize what are called results which, on the whole, are made up of facts, ordered and classified with no mention of how they were gathered."[1] In the literature on administration most of the writing is not even concerned with results in the form of observed and classified facts, but merely with generalisations from limited experience and with principles which in some instances are clearly stated as "axioms" or "propositions",[2] but which in most cases are nothing else but personal opinions.

There are several reasons for this state of affairs. A corporation or a public institution acquires a rather complex organizational and social structure as soon as its size has increased above a certain limit, and the scientific technique to be used for the study of such complex structures is not yet fully developed. Furthermore, the writers who try to

---

[1] W. Lloyd Warner and Paul S. Lunt, *The Social Life of a Modern Community*, New Haven 1941, p. 5.

[2] See e. g. Edwin O. Stene, "An Approach to a Science of Administration", *The American Political Science Review*, Vol. XXXIV (1940), pp. 1124 ff.

develop administrative theory have not always learned the hard scientific discipline "that all theories must be tested and re-tested against observed facts, and those which prove wrong ruthlessly rejected".[1] In many cases they have not had the chance to get inside the organization in order to verify their theorizing by direct observations. Other writers who as management consultants or as practical administrators have been in a position to observe the institutions from the inside have generally lacked the theoretical and scientific training to utilize their experience for anything else than the statement of simple rules of thumb. But even when they have had the necessary theoretical background their job has been to get quick results from their analyses and not to speculate on or experiment with underlying controlling factors.

For a scientific approach in administrative studies, Gulick says, the following requirements must be fulfilled:

"1. Analysis of phenomena from which we may derive standard nomenclature, measurable elements, and national concepts;

2. The development of extensive scientific documentation based upon these analyses, and

3. The encouragement of imaginative approach to social phenomena, and the publication of hypotheses so that they may be scrutinized by others in the light of experience, now and in future years."[2]

These requirements imply first of all that the laws or principles we arrive at must be founded on empirical documentation. "The development of documentation is essential . . . because it is the first step in accumulating sufficient data to submerge unimportant variables, and thus to furnish

---

[1] Colin Clark, *The Conditions of Economic Progress,* London 1940, p. VIII.

[2] Luther Gulick, "Science, Values and Public Administration" in Luther Gulick and L. Urwick (ed.), *Papers on the Science of Administration,* New York 1937, p. 194.

the basis of rational analysis".[1] But before we go out in the field in order to make our observations we must know what to look for and how to describe and measure the things we observe. That is, we must have both certain working hypotheses and certain standard concepts which will make it possible to describe the thing we observe and to test our hypotheses against our findings. Without such a conceptual framework there would be no way of selecting among the infinite number of factual observations which can be made about any concrete phenomena. But these concepts must be operational concepts, and in the reporting of our fact finding we must state the operations by which our data are arrived at.[2] "Research is fundamentally a learning process for the scientist who does it; if what he learns is to be successfully transmitted to others, he must be able to communicate how and why he did it. Those who understand are then able to test his methods and conclusions by repeating what he did."[3]

It has been our ambition in this study of the work of managing directors to plan our research and to report our findings in such a way that the conclusions we arrive at can be tested by further experience. To adopt the operational point of view implies, as Bridgman has pointed out,[4] that our task in some respects becomes simpler. We do not have to deal with a lot of questions which cannot be answer-

---

[1] *Ibid.* p. 195.

[2] Bridgman illustrates the use of operational concepts by considering the concept of length. "We evidently know what we mean by length", he says, "if we can tell what the length of any and every object is, and for the physicist nothing more is required. To find the length of an object, we have to perform certain physical operations. The concept of length is therefore fixed when the operations by which length is measured are fixed: that is, the concept of length involves as much and nothing more than the set of operations by which length is determined. In general we mean by any concept nothing more than a set of operations; *the concept is synonymous with the corresponding set of operations.*" P. W. Bridgman, *The Logic of Modern Physics,* New York 1927, p. 5.

[3] Warner and Lunt, *op. cit.* p. 6.

[4] P. W. Bridgman, *op. cit.* pp. 28—31.

ed, since there exists no way of finding the operations by which answers may be given. In other respects our task becomes more difficult, since the operational implications of the questions we want to answer are often rather involved. As will be found later, our study is very limited in its scope, and there is nothing spectacular about it. But it has been carried out in the hope that, at least on some points, it would increase our knowledge both of research methodology and of the research subject itself.

## 3. THE JOB OF THE MANAGING DIRECTOR

The first difficulty one meets in an observational study of executive work arises from the fact that this type of work is so varied and so hard to grasp. This difficulty is particularly noticeable with respect to the work of managing directors of large firms. The task is much simpler when one wants to study manual work. Let us by way of comparison take a job in forestry, e. g. the cutting down of trees. If we want to study this particular job, how do we do it?

Our *step number one* is to define what the task of cutting down trees actually implies. This task is a specialized task, and following Barnard, we may observe five different bases of specialization: (a) the place where work is done; (b) the time at which work is done; (c) the persons with whom work is done; (d) the things upon which work is done; and (e) the method or process by which work is done.[1] Observations regarding the first four of these items include studies of working conditions like weather, snow and ice situation, transport facilities etc., and the study of the working methods cover also the tools the worker has at his disposal.

After all this is done one is ready to observe the results

---

[1] Chester I. Barnard, *The Functions of the Executive*, Cambridge, Mass. 1938, pp. 127—132.

of the work, which is the *second step*. The problem here is to find practical ways of taking quantitative measurements which will without too much effort and expense show quickly and accurately how much the worker produces. Generally, a mere notation of the number of trees or the number of cubic feet is not enough. One type of tree may be more difficult to cut down than another, and snow and temperature conditions may also influence the amount of of work done.

Finally, as a *third step* there is the question of working efficiency, and this is, of course, the most important and interesting part of the whole study. We want to correlate result and effort. Here the engineers and the physiologists have developed methods by which one may measure the consumption of energy in the body during the work, the minimum amount of mechanical energy needed for the particular job, etc. In fact, a correlation may be made between the worker's consumption of food, his working effort, both measured in calories, and the quantitative result of this work.[1] Thus, to express it crudely, one may make direct comparisons between the number of ham sandwiches the worker eats and the number of trees he cuts down during a certain time period and under certain controlled conditions.

Returning to the job of the managing director, we find it, of course, much more difficult to establish reliable correlations between the amount of food they eat and the more or less wise decisions they make as heads of large business organizations. In fact, we lack the technique of measuring both the working effort and the result of the work. We may observe the working time and how it is spent, but the

---

[1] Cf. e. g. G. Luthman and N. Lundgren, "Studies of Working Methods in Swedish Forestry", *Eighth International Management Congress,* Vol. I, Stockholm 1947, pp. 149—173.

working time is not the same as the working effort; and we may notice whether the firm makes profit or not, but the amount of profit in a particular year is not necessarily a result of the managing director's effort during that year. The result of the chief executive work is a long run phenomenon, and the best we can do is to adopt the Darwinian point of view that it is the fittest who survives. The only measure of the efficiency of a co-operative system, says Barnard, is its capacity to survive.[1] If the firm has such a financial position, such equipment and working methods and such personnel and public relations that it can in the long run carry on in competition with others, we may perhaps say that the chief-executive work has been successful. Such a way of looking at the matter is, however, not particularly suited for a quantitative approach.

Fortunately, in the study of the work of the managing directors as in the study of other jobs, we need not be concerned with the *absolute* efficiency as the ratio of total result and total effort. A study of the *relative* efficiencies by a comparison of the immediate results obtained from different alternative ways of performing a specific task is generally enough.[2] In so far as we shall draw any conclusions regarding the efficiency of the behaviour we observe, the concept of efficiency will be used in this limited sense, and we shall be careful to point out how in the particular instance we define the results. Our first task, however, is what we have called step number one, an observational description of the work of the managing director.

But before we can start on our observational study of chief executive work we must know what to observe and what methods to use in our observations. One might think that the literature in the field would be of great help in

---

[1] Chester I. Barnard, *op. cit.* p. 44.

[2] Cf. Herbert A. Simon, *Administrative Behavior,* New York 1947, p. 181.

this connection, but that is not the case. This literature is more concerned with general speculations regarding the functions of the executives than with actual descriptions of their work.[1] Take, for example, Holden, Fish and Smith's definition of the function of the general management:

"The general management function may be characterized as the active planning, direction, co-ordination, and control of the business as a whole, within the scope of basic policies established and authority delegated by the board."[2]

This definition gives us some general ideas about the responsibilities of the managing director, but it says very little about what he is actually doing. Or take the conception of Fayol[3] that the chief functions of an administrator are to plan, organize, command, co-ordinate and control, which conception has been taken over in a more or less modified form by Gulick, Urwick, White and many others.[4] Again, we get here some general ideas of the tasks of the chief executives, but concepts like planning, co-ordination and control are of very limited use when we want to describe in an observational study the daily work and actual patterns of behaviour of a managing director. Most of these concepts do not fulfil the qualification of operational concepts that they should be synonymous with a clearly defined set of operations. The concept of co-ordination, for example, which is the fundamental concept in

---

[1] See e. g. R. Tannenbaum, "The Manager Concept: A Rational Synthesis", *Journal of Business of the University of Chicago,* Vol. XXII, No. 4, 1949, pp. 225 ff.

[2] Paul E. Holden, Lounsbury S. Fish and Hubert L. Smith, *Top-Management Organization and Control,* Stanford University 1941, p. 20.

[3] Henri Fayol, *Administration industrielle et générale,* Paris 1925, p. 13.

[4] Cf. e. g. Luther Gulick, "Notes on the Theory of Organization" in Gulick and Urwick, *Papers on the Science of Administration,* op. cit. p. 13, L. Urwick, *The Elements of Administration,* New York 1943, pp. 15 ff. and Leonard D. White, *Introduction to the Study of Public Administration,* 3rd ed., New York 1948, pp. 45 ff.

the best of the writing on administrative theory,[1] includes, as Gordon has pointed out, "some decision-making:
establishing broad objectives, initiating and approving
changes in key personnel and in management organization,
approving decisions on various matters in terms of the ap-
prover's interpretation of broad objectives, approving decisions on specific matters to avoid conflicts with other decisions. It also includes two other elements: the exercise of
personal leadership and the mere *possession* of authority.
The latter gives cohesion to and maintains organization, but
it does not involve any particular form of action".[2] The
concept of co-ordination does not describe *a particular set*
of operations but *all* operations which lead to a certain
result, "unity of action". If we ask a managing director
when he is co-ordinating, or how much co-ordination he
has been doing during a day he would not know, and even
the most highly skilled observer would not know either.
The same holds true of the concepts of planning, command,
organization and control, and also for most of the concepts
used by Barnard in his analysis of the executive functions.[3]

Still, we have to define the task of the managing director
in some way before we can start our empirical study. Fortunately, this can be done in very simple terms. The Report
of the President's Committee on Administrative Management states that the President of the United States, besides
being a leader of the political party in power, is "head of
the Nation in the ceremonial sense of the term, the symbol
of the American national solidarity". He also is "the Chief
Executive and administrator within the Federal system and
service.[4] Disregarding all other comparisons, we may

---

[1] Cf. e. g. Edwin O. Stene, *op. cit.*

[2] Robert Aaron Gordon, *Business Leadership in the Large Corporation,*
Washington 1945, p. 53.

[3] Cf. Chester I. Barnard, *op. cit.*

[4] *Administrative Management in the Government of the United States,*
Washington 1937, pp. 2—3.

say also of the chief executive of a business organization that he is both the symbol that has to represent his organization before the outside world, and the administrator of the organization. These two tasks have one thing, and in this connection a very important thing, in common: they both relate to people or groups of people. "The activities of individuals," says Barnard, "necessarily take place within local immediate groups. The relation of a man to a large organization, or to his nation, or to his church, is necessarily through those with whom he is in *immediate* contact. Social activities cannot be action at a distance."[1] When the managing director represents his firm before the outside world, he does so before personal representatives of this outside world, and when he administers the organization he administers the persons in the organization. One administers people, not buildings or machines. When in this study we examine the work of the managing director, it is this aspect of his work — his relationship with people — that we shall concentrate on.

## 4. PREVIOUS STUDIES

The literature on top-management is concerned with the general principles governing the way in which the executive work should be performed rather than with observational descriptions of how it is actually carried on. Nevertheless there is a certain amount of material dealing with this latter problem which is worthy of note. Unfortunately I have had to limit my research into the literature of the subject to the Scandinavian libraries, and the positive results of this research — with the exception of the works by Nolting and Lasswell mentioned below — have become available so late

---

[1] Chester I. Barnard, *op. cit.* p. 119.

that they have been of no help for the planning of the present study.

The material referred to can be classified with respect to the subject matter in two different groups. The first group, which is rather scanty, contains some data on how various types of executives spend their working day, and the second discusses methodological problems in connection with studies of executive work. To the first group belongs a study by Nolting on the work of city managers. "When 21 city managers kept for a week a daily record of the time spent on different activities", writes Nolting,[1] "they reported an average work week of 54 hours. On the basis of a six day week, their average nine-hour day was distributed as follows:

> Talking with citizens in office and over telephone — 2 hours
> Conferences with department heads — 1 ½ hours.
> Planning current activities and future work — 1 hour
> Handling correspondence — 1 hour
> Formal and informal meetings with city council — 50 minutes
> Inspecting municipal activities — 50 minutes
> Attending meetings and talking before various groups — 40 minutes
> Preparing official reports — 30 minutes
> Interviewing candidates for positions — 20 minutes
> Miscellaneous — 20 minutes".

Similar data on the distribution of the daily working time of 12 German "directors" are published in an article by W. H. in *Betriebswirtschaftliche Forschung und Praxis*.[2] The data were obtained, says the author, by an inquiry addressed to the leaders of a number of large industrial firms, but no further information is given as regards the nature and reliability of the material. The results of the inquiry were as follows:

---

[1] Orin F. Nolting, *Management Methods in City Government*, Chicago 1942, p. l., as quoted in *The Technique of Municipal Administration*, Chicago 1945, p. 4.

[2] Nr 10, 1. *Jahrgang* (1949) pp. 603—614.

| | Number of hours per day | | |
| --- | :---: | :---: | :---: |
| Conversations and conferences | Average | Maximum | Minimum |
| at the home office | 3 | 4 | 2 |
| Conversations and conferences | | | |
| outside the home office | 1½ | 3 | 1 |
| Reading of incoming mail | 1½ | 2 | 1 |
| Reading of newspapers, technical journals etc. | 1 | 2 | ½ |
| Dictating and giving of instructions to the secretary | 2 | 3 | 1 |
| Telephone conversations | ½ | 1 | ½ |
| Signing letters etc. | ½ | 1 | — |
| Total | 10 | 16 | 6 |

Mention should also be made of the *Fortune* management poll of 1946 on executive opinion regarding their own work.[1]

As regards literature on research methods in connection with executive studies I have as yet found only three works that have direct bearing on the present study. The first is a chapter by Lasswell in his book on political behaviour.[2] It contains a description of a self-observational study of the daily contact-pattern made by a bureau chief in Washington who was having serious "budget troubles". The data were assembled by continuous notations on small slips, one for every day, of all the persons with whom he came in contact during a month. "The results of this extremely simple procedure were somewhat revealing to the administrator. Well over nine in every ten contacts were with members of his own bureau — this included all waking hours in the day."[3] A similar "internalized" contact-pattern was

---

[1] Fortune XXXIV (1946), nr 4, pp. 5 ff.
[2] Harold D. Lasswell, "Self-Observation: Recording the Focus of Attention", *The Analysis of Political Behaviour, An Emperical Approach*, London 1947, pp. 279—286.
[3] *Ibid.* p. 280.

found for the executive secretary of a trade association, while a very different pattern was revealed for a college president. Lasswell gives also suggestions on how this simple self-observational technique can be developed in order to answer various questions that may arise out of material of this kind.

In his book on administrative procedure Glaser[1] describes a method for measuring executive work load in a government office. Under this method each executive had during a test period to enter on a daily report card a running record of his activities. The record showed

the time consumed on each item of work,
the "type of work", such as conferences, telephone calls, reading and writing or dictating,
the place of work; with the subheadings "own office" and "other office",
the person contacted, and
the subject matter.

As will be seen in the next chapter of this book, we used a rather similar set of concepts in the present study, which was developed without any knowledge of Glaser's work.

Glaser does not mention how far such studies have actually been carried out and what the findings were. He gives, however, several suggestions as to how such an investigation technique can be used in determining "how much time could be saved by having certain subjects handled by subordinates, by having certain officials deal with each other directly instead of through the officer in question, and by various other specific rearrangements".[2] He also describes how the data can be used for a sociometric study of the communication patterns inside the organization.

---

[1] Comstock Glaser, *Administrative Procedure,* Washington 1947, pp. 32—36.
[2] *Ibid.* p. 34.

Of still greater interest in connection with the present study is the research program on "Leadership in Democracy" which is in progress at the Ohio State University. Thus far very little seems to have been published regarding these studies. The only thing that has come to my notice is one article by Shartle in *Personnel*[1] and another by Stogdill in *Sociometry*,[2] both of 1949. Shartle describes some of the methods used in "the study of administrative positions in business, industry, the armed services, and education". When studying the behaviour of the persons assumed to be performing leadership acts and of the organizations they work with, the following sets of variables are observed:

1. The general background, such as the history of the group and of the individual members of the group.

2. The situation in which leadership acts occur. This includes the organizational structure, the present goals of the organization and the formal and informal status of the leaders within the structure.

3. The leadership acts themselves, "what the leader does". "About 200 persons have been studied in 10 structures. Job analysis, which has had wide use and which if properly utilized seems to provide reliable data, has been applied. This involves the observation of the member of the organization, a review of his communications, conferences with his associates in the organization, and a noting of the interpersonal relationships involved in carrying out the functions of the organization."[3] The leadership activities were classified in 14 groups:

inspection of the organization,
investigation and research,

[1] Carroll L. Shartle, "Leadership and Executive Performance", *Personnel*, XXV (1949) pp. 370—380.
[2] Ralph M. Stogdill, "The Sociometry of Working Relationships in Formal Organizations", Sociometry, XII (1949) pp. 276—286.
[3] *Ibid*. p. 375.

planning,
preparation of procedures and methods,
coordination,
evaluation,
interpretation of plans and procedures,
supervision of technical operations,
personnel activities,
public relations,
professional consultation,
negotiations,
scheduling, routing and dispatching, and
technical and professional operations.

By the use of questionnaire and interview methods each person studied was got to indicate the proportion of the time he spent on each one of these activities. Thus a "quantitative" pattern was obtained for every person. Although the present writer from his own experience has become somewhat sceptical as regards the utility of some of the concepts used in this description of leadership activities, the value of a conceptual framework can only be judged by the results that are obtained in the final analysis, and these results are not yet available.

In the study of the interpersonal relationships inside the organizations various types of sociometric charts are employed in a most effective and interesting manner. Some preliminary results from this part of the study are mentioned both by Shartle and by Stogdill in the article in *Sociometry*. What has been published so far regarding this research program seems very promising indeed, and one awaits the forthcoming results with great interest.

*Chapter 2*

# DEVELOPING A METHOD

> The Method I take to do this is not very usual; for
> instead of using only comparative and superlative words,
> and intellectual arguments, I have taken the course (as a
> specimen of the Political Arithmetic I have long aimed
> at) to express myself in terms of Number, Weight, or
> Measure; to use only arguments of sense, and to consider
> only such causes, as have visible foundations in nature;
> leaving those that depend upon the mutable minds,
> opinions, appetites, and passions of particular men, to
> the consideration of others.
>
> *Sir William Petty*

## 1. THE SCOPE OF THE STUDY

Executive behaviours can be studied both in their relation to psychological or mental systems or in their
relation to social systems. The former type of study is the
task of the psychologists and the latter the task of the social
scientists. As an example of a psychological study of executive behaviour I may mention the work of William Henry
and his associates at the University of Chicago.[1] In his
investigation of American business executives Henry tries
to relate their success or failure to certain common personal-
ity characteristics, such as acquisitiveness, self-directedness,

---

[1] William E. Henry, "The Business Executive: The Psycho-Dynamics
of a Social Role", *"The American Journal of Sociology"*, Vol. LIV (1949)
pp. 286—291. For a comprehensive review of current psychological research in relation to executive work see R. M. Stogdill, "Personnel Factors
Associated with Leadership", *Journal of Psychology*, Vol. 25 (1948), pp.
35—71.

decisiveness etc. The present study, on the other hand, is a study of executive behaviours in their relation to other human beings in a particular social structure. It is a study in the field of social science. The social structure is the Swedish society with its government institutions, its trade associations, its business firms etc., and the most relevant part of this structure for the study is, of course, the business organization, of which the executive is the managing director.

As was mentioned in the first chapter, the study aims at certain practical results. It may therefore be labelled as a piece of practical research. But there is no fundamental distinction between practical and theoretical research. If theoretical propositions cannot be applied in practice for the prediction of future events, it is bad theory. On the other hand, if by practical research we can arrive at knowledge which helps us to predict the outcome of certain human behaviour, this knowledge is of importance also for our theoretical understanding.[1]

In the present state of knowledge our primary task has been to devise and test a method for an observational description of executive work. In so far as we have succeeded with this task, that will be our most important result. But what we want is an observation technique that will not only help us to describe the actual work of the business executive, but will also be a useful instrument for the detection of deficiencies in his work. We want to devise better methods of diagnosis for the administrative clinician.

The number of individual cases studied was ten, nine in Sweden and one in France, but this report will mainly be concerned with the Swedish cases. With such limited material at our disposal, and with cases which were purposely selected from firms in different stages of development,

---

[1] Cf. Arnold M. Rose, "The Selection of Problems for Research", *The American Journal of Sociology,* Vol. LIV (1948), p. 220.

with different organizational structure, and in different industries, a statistical analysis of the "typical" or "average" behaviour of the executives was out of the question. We treated every case individually and the analyses of the individual behaviours were made separately.

## 2. OPERATIONAL CONCEPTS

As a frame of reference we devised a set of operational concepts rather similar to Barnard's system of specialization, mentioned above. His first and third bases of specialization:

(a) the place where work is done, and
(c) the people with whom work is done,

we also used. His fourth and fifth bases:

(d) the things upon which work is done, and
(e) the methods or process by which work is done,

we formulated in a somewhat different way, distinguishing the technique of communication used in contacting people, the nature of the questions that are brought up before the managing director, and the kind of action he takes with regard to these questions. Thus for every executive action we tried to collect data on:

I.   Place of work
II.  Contact with persons and institutions
III. Technique of communication
IV.  Nature of question handled
V.   Kind of action.

Before I comment further on these bases of classification, I shall say a few words regarding Barnard's second base:

(b) the time at which work is done.

The element of time was brought into our study in two different ways. *Firstly,* we had to select a specific time period, during which the observational recording of the executive behaviour would take place. I shall discuss that problem in a later section of this chapter. *Secondly,* the time together with the frequency was our main unit of measurement. We tried to observe the actual time used in every contact and for every particular piece of work. By doing so we regarded time units as homogeneous units irrespective of what they were used for and when they took place. Thus, a ten-minute review of reports was regarded as one and the same operation, whether it was made in the morning, when the executive's brain was thoroughly rested, or late at night after a long and tiring working day.

Let us now return to our system of classification and see how this was applied in the observational study.

I. *Place of work.* The mere recording of the place of work gave us some idea of what the managing director was doing, or rather what he was not doing. If we found, for example, that he spent his whole day in his office, we knew that he was not on an inspection tour in the plant. If he was attending a conference outside the firm, the mere observation of where this conference was held also often gave us some notion of his duties.

II. *Contacts with persons and institutions.* Starting out with the conception that the main task of the executive is to administer his own people and to represent the firm vis-à-vis other people, the recording of the people he met in his daily work became perhaps the most important part of the whole study. It may be mentioned that the managing directors we have studied thus far spent between 65 and 90 per cent of their total working time in contact with other people. These people included not only the firms' own staff and the members of their boards of directors, but also all the persons from outside with whom they had to deal as the chief representatives of their firms.

III. *Technique of communication.* "I believe", says Elton Mayo, "that social study should begin with careful observations of what may be described as communication; that is, the capacity for an individual to communicate his feelings and ideas to another, the capacity of groups to communicate effectively and intimately to each other."[1] By technique of communication we mean here the methods used by the executive in order to get into contact with the people and the institutions he has to deal with. It describes how he obtains information from others and how he himself conveys ideas to other people. For the sake of simplicity we have also included under this heading the technique of getting information by direct observation, e. g. during an inspection tour in the plant.

IV. *Nature of question handled.* The concepts thus far discussed were useful also for the study of what questions the executives had to deal with in their daily work. The statistics of the distribution of their working time with respect to various places of work, of their contacts with institutions and people inside and outside the firm, of their attendance at committee meetings and of the reports they received gave us some ideas about the material contents of their work. In fact during the first stage of our investigation, this was the only data we collected. Our working hypothesis was that a mere observation of the personal contacts would also enable us to draw some conclusions regarding the nature of the questions brought up. We simply assumed that if, for example, the managing director had a talk with the sales manager, the issue discussed was a question of sales.

---

[1] Elton Mayo, *The Social Problems of an Industrial Civilization*, New York 1945, p. 22.

The limitations of such an approach are obvious. The main task of the chief executive is, of course, not to consider a problem in its "functional" but in its company-wide aspects. Thus, a question brought to him by the sales manager may very well be classified as a sales problem from the point of view of the latter, but from the point of view of the managing director it may just as well be a problem that touches manufacturing, financing or personnel, and should be classified accordingly. If the problem had no other aspects than sales, it would in most cases never have been referred to the chief executive's consideration. Furthermore, from a mere observation of his contacts we shall never find out either what the managing director does when he works by himself, or which problems he specially wants to talk to other people about. During the later stage of our study we observed that there may be some questions, e. g. personnel questions, that the chief executive wants to discuss with all his subordinates. If we were to assume in such a case that personnel problems are only discussed in the presence of the personnel manager, our conclusions would, of course, be completely wrong.

In order to avoid these shortcomings we introduced during the later stage of our investigation a series of concepts relating to the nature of the question handled. We were here forced to abandon the purely observational approach and to introduce continous interviews as a supplement to the behaviouristic study.

*Firstly,* we classified the questions the executive dealt with according to what might be called their material contents or field of activity. Since the main activities of the firms were delegated to the first and second line subordinates according to a definite plan based on "functions" such as manufacturing or marketing, on geographical location or on products or services, we generally adopted this plan for our classifications. Thus for this aspect of the problem we used a separate classification system for each individual study.

*Secondly,* we classified the questions dealt with as questions of development or questions of current operation. It is often said that the primary task of the chief executive is to look to the future of the firm. The questions he is dealing with should consequently cover future developments rather than current operations. A test of this hypothesis against actual observations was one of the goals we set before us.

*Thirdly,* we classified the questions handled as questions of policy or questions of application. When a question is brought up to the chief executive for consideration, this is often done in order that a precedent shall be established for future actions. The establishment of such precedents or "policies"[1] is one of the chief ways for an executive to diminish his own working load. Since the conditions under which the firm is carrying out its business are continually changing, the formation of new policies and the adaptation of existing policies to new circumstances is an never-ending task.

In summary the nature of the question handled was classified in three different ways:

with regard to the material contents of the questions (the field of activity), with sub-classes chosen individually for every particular firm;

with regard to questions of development and questions of current operation; and

with regard to questions of policy and questions of application.

---

[1] "A business *policy,* as I understand it", writes Copeland, "is a general rule of action which is developed, either formally or informally, for guiding members of an organization in deciding specific questions within the range of the policy as they arise under changing conditions." Melvin T. Copeland, "The Job of an Executive", *Harvard Business Review,* XVIII (1940) p. 155.

V. *Kind of action.* Our curiosity did not end when we had acquired a knowledge of the nature of the questions dealt with by the chief executives. We also wanted to know what they did about these questions. In simple terms one may perhaps say that the main task of an executive is

to take decisions or to see to it that decisions are taken by others, and

to make sure that these decisions are carried out by the members of his organization.

In order to take decisions he needs information and it is also necessary for him to systematize this information so that he will arrive at a decision. It is, I suppose, this phase of his work that in management literature often is referred to as "planning". The carrying out of the decisions involves on the part of the executive the giving of orders, advising and explaining, and inspection and review. But there are also other "kinds of action" to be found in the work of the chief executive. There are certain matters which he has to execute himself; e. g. to show the works to distinguished visitors, to give speeches or to distribute prizes on special occasions. He also spends some time on his personal development. To a certain extent this is a question of getting information, but that does not cover all aspects of the problem.

In our observational study the kinds of actions, consequently, were classified under the following subheadings:

getting information
systematizing information
taking decisions
confirming or correcting the decisions of others
giving orders
advising and explaining
inspecting and reviewing
executing
personal development.

There are several critical comments to be made regarding this list of concepts, but before I embark on such a critique I want to review some of the problems of recording and classification.

## 3. RECORDING AND CLASSIFICATION OF DATA

It should be remembered that the main part of this study took place in firms with which I had been connected for several years, and about which I already had a great deal of information. This information was, of course, of great help both when I had to plan the collection and classification of my new data and when these data were finally analysed. The problem of collecting data was that the recording must not interfere with or influence the executives' usual behaviour patterns; and I think that we were rather successful in this respect. The recording technique used varied with the nature of the data. Some data were collected by the chief executives' private secretaries or their personal assistants, by the telephone exchange operators and the porters, and one of my assistant's chief tasks in connection with the collecting of data was to train these people in the recording technique to be used. Other data were recorded immediately by the chief executives themselves, while for other parts of our study we got the necessary information through extensive interviews with the chief executives, their private secretaries and other persons in their immediate surroundings who had an intimate knowledge of their working patterns.

### Place of work and personal contacts

The recording of the time the chief executive spent in various places of work and in personal contact with people visiting him at his office was generally done by his private secretary. A special form was supplied for this purpose (see fig. 1), of which one part was to be filled in for the morning period, and another for the afternoon period and the evening. When the secretary could not observe the relevant

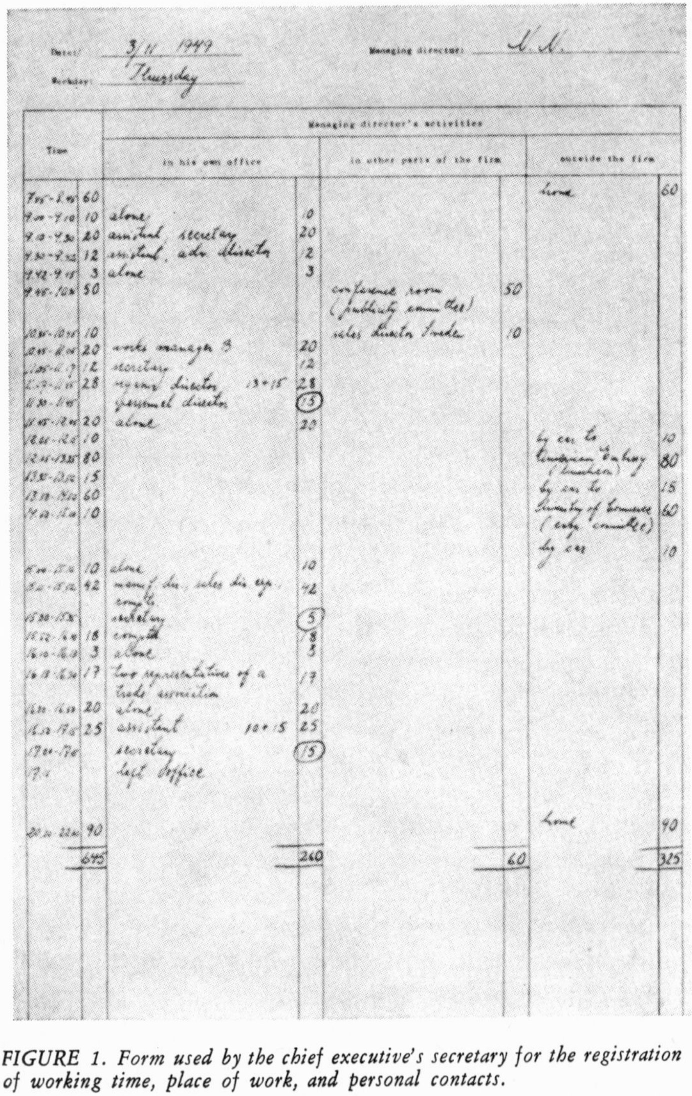

FIGURE 1. *Form used by the chief executive's secretary for the registration of working time, place of work, and personal contacts.*

events herself she obtained the necessary information from the porter, the telephone exchange operator or the chief executive himself. If, for example, the managing director left his office for the day in the early afternoon in order to attend a meeting outside the firm, the secretary would ask him the next morning when the meeting ended and if he had done any other work after the meeting. A similar recording of all incoming and outgoing telephone calls was made on another form by the telephone exchange operator. Finally the private secretary prepared a list of all letters dictated and signed by the chief executive.

Although with the aid of this recording technique we got fairly complete information regarding the time distribution of the executives' work with reference to the place of work and the contacts he had with persons and institutions, there were some deficiencies in the recording which should be noticed. Thus we never succeeded in recording all the personal contacts the executive had outside his office, e. g. when he made an inspection tour in a plant or when he attended a meeting outside the firm. It was also difficult to get a complete record of the telephone calls with respect to both their frequency and their duration — particularly the latter. This was especially the case with the internal calls, and where a conference telephone was used, we could merely observe which persons could be reached by this telephone. Fortunately the conference telephone was used mostly in order to fix for appointments or for matters where only a quick answer was needed on a special question, and seldom for conversations of any length.

Another item which was difficult to record completely was the executives' working time outside the firm. As was mentioned above, the executive had to report this work daily to his secretary, but it was not always so easy for him to decide what activities he ought to regard as work. Was reading of memoranda and trade journals work only when it was done in his office or without disturbance at his home in the evenings, or was it also when he did it in the train going to and from his office? Was it work when he discussed the firm's affairs with a colleague or a subordinate during a Sunday walk? We never tried to formulate any rules for the judgment of these questions, but left them for the individual executives to decide for themselves.

As a consequence of these shortcomings in our recording technique, it became difficult to get an exact measurement both of the executives' total working time and of the part of their working time when they were undisturbed by visits and telephone calls. When for example we computed the time for "working alone in his office", the results meant that the executive had been undisturbed by visitors, but it did not mean — except in a few cases — that he had been undisturbed by telephone calls.

The classification system used for the data relating to the place of work was the following:

Inside the firm:    1. own office
                    2. other parts of head-office
                    3. other parts of home plant
                    4. visits to other of the firm's plants
Outside the firm:   5. at home
                    6. other places (to be specified).

With the exception of the difficulties with the recording of the work outside the firm mentioned above, there were no problems of classification. Such problems arose, however, when we started to classify the data relating to the executive's personal contacts. There were few difficulties about the contacts the executive had with the people inside the firm, the members of the board of directors or the subordinates. These contacts could be classified on the basis of existing organization charts. There were some difficulties about how to measure the duration of individual contacts when the executive met several people at the same time, e. g. when someone came in to his office while he already had other visitors, or when someone visited him while he was sitting in a committee meeting. The main classification difficulties related, however, to his contacts with people outside the firm. The headings under which these outside contacts were classified were generally the following:

1. Official authorities
2. Trade associations, chambers of commerce etc.
3. Scientific institutions
4. Trade unions and employers' federations
5. Other companies of which the chief executive was a member of the board
6. Customers
7. Suppliers
8. Banks and representatives of financial institutions
9. Outside companies
10. Private visitors
11. Others.

In some cases additional headings were introduced for such categories as "outside consultants" or "colleagues from foreign countries". It was not always so easy to decide in which category to place a particular contact. The contacts recorded were contacts with persons, and the same person might represent more than one class. There is, for instance, no clear borderline between official authorities and trade associations or employers' federations. An executive in such an association may be a member of a government committee, as also a member of any of the other categories listed may be. Furthermore, when the executive attends, say, a meeting in his employers' association, he comes in contact with people who may be his customers or suppliers etc. In order to get a complete picture of the executives' outside contacts one would need to have information regarding the contents of every conversation they had, both inside and outside their firms. As will be described later, we generally collected such information only with respect to visits made by outside people to the executives' own offices.

*Technique of communication*

The technique of communication, as I have said, is the technique used by the executive in order to obtain information from, and convey ideas to, the people he is in contact with. We may here distinguish the following subclasses:

Direct contacts:
1. personal observations (e. g. during an inspection tour)
2. conversations, person to person
3. conferences — regular and *ad hoc*
4. telephone calls

Indirect contacts:
5. via persons (e. g. staff assistants, private secretaries etc.)
6. via papers (which the executive reads or writes).

A great deal of information regarding the use of these different communication techniques could be obtained from the data on the executive's contacts, mentioned above. These data told us, for example, how much time he spent on inspection tours to various parts of the firm, or in formal and *ad hoc* conferences. They also told us when he made use of letter writing, telephone calls or personal appointments. Additional information regarding the communication technique was obtained by collection of data for a full year on internal committees and conferences, on internal control reports etc. Thus we made a systematic survey of all the committee meetings and conferences inside the firm in which the chief executive regularly took part, recording how the meetings were announced, how they were planned and run, if minutes were kept, etc. We made another survey of all the reports which were read regularly by the chief executive, recording their size, main contents and periodicity. In addition we learned about the technique used with respect to personal appointments, telephone calls and correspondence and private reading, from interwievs with the private secretary, the telephone exchange operator and the chief executive himself.

### *Nature of question handled and kind of action*

In order to find out what questions the chief executives actually dealt with in their daily work and what actions they made in relation to these questions, we had to ask the executives themselves. Our technique was as follows: We designed a standardized questionnaire, sized about $4'' \times 5\frac{1}{2}''$, which we spread all round the executive. He had copies of the questionnaire on his desk, in his pocket, at his home etc. The headings contained on this questionnaire (see fig. 2) were the following:

1. *date,*
2. *time,*
3. *telephone call,* with appropriate space for noting incoming and outgoing calls,
4. *place of work;* annotations were made only if the place of work was other than the executive's own office,
5. *person contacted;* in order to simplify the annotations, symbols were given for the persons with whom the executive was in contact most frequently. Otherwise it was sufficient if the executive marked the initials of the person in question, which would permit his identification on the form kept for daily activities (fig. 1) mentioned above,
6. *nature of question handled,* with sub-headings with regard to
   A. the fields of activity
   B. questions of development and of current operations, and

[45]

C. questions of policy and of application; and

7. *kinds of action,* with the sub-headings described above.

For every personal appointment, conference or telephone

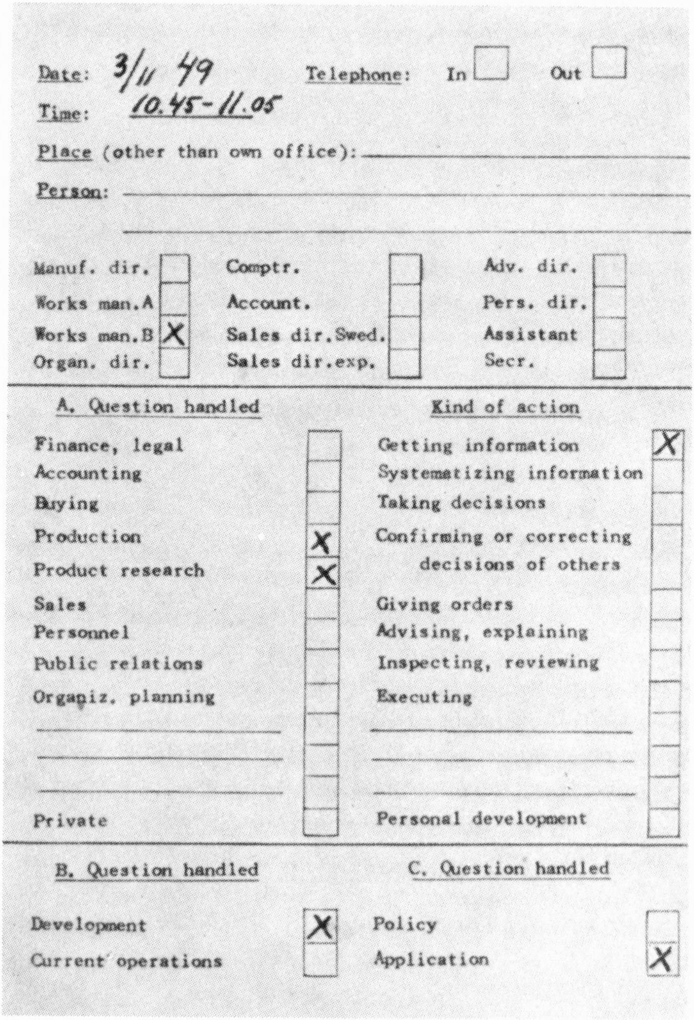
Date: 3/11 49    Telephone: In [ ] Out [ ]

Time: 10.45–11.05

Place (other than own office): ______

Person: ______

| | | | | | |
|---|---|---|---|---|---|
| Manuf. dir. | [ ] | Comptr. | [ ] | Adv. dir. | [ ] |
| Works man. A | [ ] | Account. | [ ] | Pers. dir. | [ ] |
| Works man. B | X | Sales dir. Swed. | [ ] | Assistant | [ ] |
| Organ. dir. | [ ] | Sales dir. exp. | [ ] | Secr. | [ ] |

| A. Question handled | | Kind of action | |
|---|---|---|---|
| Finance, legal | [ ] | Getting information | X |
| Accounting | [ ] | Systematizing information | [ ] |
| Buying | [ ] | Taking decisions | [ ] |
| Production | X | Confirming or correcting decisions of others | [ ] |
| Product research | X | | |
| Sales | [ ] | Giving orders | [ ] |
| Personnel | [ ] | Advising, explaining | [ ] |
| Public relations | [ ] | Inspecting, reviewing | [ ] |
| Organiz. planning | [ ] | Executing | [ ] |
| ______ | [ ] | ______ | [ ] |
| ______ | [ ] | ______ | [ ] |
| ______ | [ ] | ______ | [ ] |
| Private | [ ] | Personal development | [ ] |

| B. Question handled | | C. Question handled | |
|---|---|---|---|
| Development | X | Policy | [ ] |
| Current operations | [ ] | Application | X |

*FIGURE 2. Standardized questionnaire used by the chief executives themselves for the recording of nature of questions handled and kind of action.*

call, and for every question the chief executive worked on for himself, he was asked to tick the appropriate headings on this questionnaire. After a short introductory training this task was done in a few seconds, and it in no way interfered with his ordinary work. (In fact, some of the directors got so used to filling in these questionnaires, that they complained when at the end of the investigation period they were not supplied with more forms!) Twice a day the questionnaires were collected by the private secretary or an assistant, who had to check them against the forms used for registering visitors and telephone calls. Naturally the quality of the data thus obtained varied as between different individual studies, but at least in five of the seven cases where this technique was used, the questionnaires returned to us were quite complete and very conscientiously marked.

These data regarding the nature of the questions handled and the kind of actions taken are, however, of a different kind from the data previously described. While we could register the actual behaviour of the chief executive with respect to place of work and personal contacts what we register here is not the executive's behaviour but their *opinions* about their behaviour. The opinions are expressed in standardized terms and they are registered almost simultaneously with the corresponding actions, which makes them very useful, but as with all opinions, they relate to particular persons at a particular instant of time. Thus, it becomes very difficult to make comparisons of the questions handled and the actions taken as between different executives. What one may hope for is merely that the individual executive will be consistent enough in his own marking for comparisons to be made as between the nature of the questions discussed with different people or the kind of actions taken for different types of questions. Since we did not expect to make any interpersonal comparisons, it was not necessary for us to define the concepts to be used in an exact way. We could leave it to the executive himself to decide within rather wide margins how he wanted to classify the particular items.

While the executives generally had no difficulty in classifying what fields of activity an individual question related to, or whether it was a question of development or current operations, they said that in many cases it was rather difficult to decide whether it was a question of policy or of application. There is no clear borderline between these concepts. One may think at the beginning of a discussion that the item brought up is merely a trifling detail, while further consideration reveals that the decision taken turns out to be a most important precedent for the future. Nevertheless, every scrap of actual information regarding this aspect of executive work is, of course, most welcome.

In the analysis of the data relating to the nature of questions handled, we got — among other things — into the following difficulty. It often happened that the chief executive classified a question under several different headings. An item discussed with a sous-chef could e. g. be marked as "manufacturing" and "finance", "development" and "current operation" and "policy". Whether in such a case there were actually two different subjects that were discussed during the same visit, or one subject which had all these aspects, we never knew. At the final stage of the study we got one of the executives to make out a separate form for every separate item he worked on and not only one form for every visit etc., but he said that it was generally very difficult to decide whether and when the conversation shifted from one item to another. This weakness in our investigation technique prevented us from drawing any but very tentative conclusions regarding the frequency of "company-wide" questions as compared with questions of a purely "functional" character, a study which, of course, would have been very interesting to make.

The study of the kind of action was, as I expected it to be, the most difficult part of our whole investigation, and neither the concepts nor the recording technique used are as yet sufficiently refined in this respect. Nevertheless the data obtained were most valuable. They clearly showed, for instance, that for the chief executive the main problems were those of "getting information" and "advising and explaining". In their own opinion, most of the directors studied did not take part in so very many decisions and it was seldom that they gave orders. It is probable, however, that if we had asked the subordinates to mark down the kind of actions taken, the picture might have been quite different. A conversation which from the point of view of the managing director merely means the getting of information may very well be regarded by the subordinates as decision-taking or even the receiving of orders.

It seems to me that our knowledge of this aspect of the executive work would have been much more complete if we had classified the nature of the questions handled with respect to their time aspect also. By that I mean whether the particular question related to a coming or a past event. When for exemple the executive "gets information" regarding something which has not yet happened, this seems to have more of a directive significance than if the event has already taken place. In general the concepts used for describing various kinds of actions only get an exact meaning when they are clearly related to the time aspect of the question on which action is taken. Unfortunately this was not done.

### Complementary data

As a complement to the observational study thus far described, we carried out a fairly extensive interview programme, which included not only the chief executives themselves but also their secretaries and other persons inside their organization who had first-hand knowledge of their daily behaviour patterns. The interviews were generally semi-directed, there were some definite topics which we wanted to bring up, but they were complemented by a series of free conversations. We also collected data regarding

the formal organization plans of the firms,

the localization and size of the various plants,

the local amenities and the internal system of communication of the head offices,

the associations, boards and outside committees the executives were members of,

the number of meetings these various institutions had had during the last 12 months,

the number of days the executives had been away from their firms during the same period, etc.

For the Swedish part of the study, we made use, of course, of all the material we had collected in earlier studies of the firms' formal and informal organization and their policies with respect to various aspects of their activity.

### 4. THE SELECTION OF THE OBSERVATION PERIOD

One of the difficulties in a study of chief executive work is that this work varies so much as between different seasons and different years. Thus, the selection of a representative observation period is no easy task. At the beginning of the year, before the annual report to the stockholders is published, the chief executive generally spends much more time on accounting matters than during the rest of the year. Before and during a wage negotiation he concentrates on wage and production problems, and before and during a sales conference on questions of marketing and advertising. But not only that. One year the negotiation of a contract with a trade union may go on very smoothly without the intervention of the chief executive, while another year he may himself spend days or weeks on such a question. His work also varies according to his own particular stage of development, that of his nearest subordinates, and that of his organization in general. To get a really reliable picture of his work from a study of a rather limited period is well-nigh impossible. Still, that was what we had to do.

Since some of the data we wanted had to be continuously supplied by the chief executives themselves, we had to limit our investigation period to a rather short time. In all cases but one the study period was four weeks. We thought that to extend the study over more than four weeks would cause the quality of our data to deteriorate. In fact, in a few cases the data supplied diminished in completeness and precision even after a week or two, while in other cases it was of the same high standard on the last day of the observational study as on the first. This limitation of our investigation period was, of course, one of our main obstacles. Fortunately, however, there are some aspects of the managing directors' work which are fairly independent of seasonal and cyclical variations. Such matters as whether an executive generally limits his personal contacts inside his organization to a few people at the top or prefers to see a large number of his subordinates, whether he prefers formal conferences to *ad hoc* visits, whether he likes to work with a large number of statistical reports or not, are more influenced by the character of the man himself or of the organization he works in than temporary external conditions.

As in all studies in the field of social relations we had to be on our guard against the possibility that the mere existence of the study might influence the behaviour of our research object. In how far the daily working patterns of the chief executives were changed consciously or unconsciously because they were observed, we do not actually know, but all the evidence we have indicates that the change was not great. In several respects we could check the data collected for the observation period against similar data covering a full year, and also against the evidence obtained from the interviews with subordinates. Indeed, even had the executives wanted to change their behaviour, they did not have much chance to do so. The content of their working day is determined only to a small extent by themselves, and it is difficult to change it without making considerable alterations in the organizational structure of which they are parts. Before we made the study, I always thought of a chief executive as the conductor of an orchestra, standing aloof on his platform. Now I am in some respects inclined to see him as the puppet in a puppet-show with hundreds of people pulling the strings and forcing him to act in one way or another.

*Chapter 3*

# THE EXECUTIVES AND THEIR
# SOCIAL ENVIRONMENT

C'est dans l'imitation qu'il faut chercher la raison de
la plupart des actions humaines. En se conformant à la
coutume on passera toujours pour un honnête homme.
On appelle gens de bien ceux qui font comme les
autres.

*Anatole France*

## 1. THE EXECUTIVE GROUP

In order to understand the executive behaviours in their
relation to human beings in a social structure, it is necessary to know some characteristics of this structure. Before I
report some of the findings of our study I shall therefor try
to outline some characteristic features of the executive group
in Swedish industry, of the organizational structure of the
firms in which the executives work, and of the relationships
between these firms and society at large.

If we go back to the last decades of the nineteenth
century, we find an executive group in Swedish industry
consisting primarily of merchants. The merchant class do-
minated not only trade, shipping and banking, but also most
of the branches of industry proper. The main exception was
in the iron and steel industry, which has a long tradition in
the country and where the executives were industrialists in
the ordinary meaning of the word. In industry as a whole,
however, the training of young men who expected to reach
the executive level was mainly a practical one. After having

finished the general education stipulated by law, they might spend a few years at a secondary school or at a business school or technical institute, but in most cases they went directly into industry. Business executives with a university degree were an exceedingly rare species. If one could afford it, it was regarded as much more valuable to spend some years as an apprentice in a merchant house in London or Hamburg than to go to a university.

Today the situation is quite different. The developments which have taken place in the last 50 or 60 years in the fields of production and marketing technique, of business organization, of politics and economics have produced business leaders of an entirely new type. The men with a practical merchant training have been superseded by people with a university education, who have started their practical career not as general apprentices but as functional specialists in large firms. In order to get some factual data on this development I made a study some years ago of the theoretical and practical training of 200 managing directors and deputy managing directors in leading Swedish business firms.[1] It is a rather limited sample, but I believe it gives a fairly representative picture of the present situation. The conclusions drawn are supported by the evidence from a similar sample study made by one of my former students.[2]

If we first look at the antecedents of these executives, from the data at my disposal it was only possible to get information regarding the profession of their fathers, and this only for 180 out of the 200. In 57 per cent of the cases the father's profession was stated simply as business man, in 35 per cent as civil servant or staff employee in private firms, in 7 per cent as farmer and only in 1 per cent as workman. While, as I have mentioned earlier, the business

---

[1] Cf. Sune Carlson, *Företagsledning och företagsledare*, Stockholm 1945, pp. 99—105 and 150—157.
[2] B. Hökby, "Om företagsledare i storindustrin", *Balans*, Vol. II (1950), pp. 97 ff.

executives of fifty years ago were in most cases merchants, it seems as if today they are sons of merchants.

A study of the theoretical training of the 200 executives in the sample reveals that 104 have university degrees, most of them in engineering, business administration or law, and 45 are graduates of technical institutes or business schools of various types. The percentage of university trained men is, as one might expect, considerably higher among the younger executives than among the older. If we divide the material into two age-groups with 55 years as a dividing line, we get 107 in the younger group, of whom 67 have had university training, while the corresponding figures for the older group are 93 and 37.[1] As regards their practical training, more than 60 per cent of the total group have had their main career inside one single firm. Those who have had leading positions in firms in more than one branch of industry constitute not more than 15 per cent. The professional administrator, who goes from one chief executive job to another, is still a rather unusual phenomenon in Swedish industry.

If we return for a moment to the nine managing directors whose behaviour patterns are the object of this present study, I may mention that they are all university graduates. One of them has degrees both in arts and in law, and two have degrees in science, two in law, two in engineering and two in business administration. As regards their practical training, six of them have had their main career in the firms where they now are managing directors, while two have had leading positions in several firms in different branches of industry. One was in the civil service until he got his present job as managing director of an insurance company a few years ago.

[1] The same tendency was found by Taussig and Joslyn in their extensive study of American business executives at the beginning of the 1930's. Cf. F. W. Taussig and C. S. Joslyn, *American Business Leaders,* New York, 1932, p. 164.

If we confine the executive group to the managing directors of the leading 200 or 500 business firms in the Swedish economy, this group seems in most respects to be much more homogeneous than the corresponding groups in countries like the United States, Great Britain or France. There are several reasons for this homogeneity. We have already mentioned the similarity in the extraction, the education and the practical career of the members of the group. We must also remember the small size of the Swedish community. The executives not only belong to the same alumni associations or professional or social organizations, they meet each other regularly in all sorts of affairs. They sit on the same government committees, the same boards in employers' federations, trade associations and chambers of commerce, they use the same large banks as their financial associates, and so on. Often they are members of the boards of directors in each others' firms. All this produces a strong feeling of solidarity or group consciousness among the members of the executive group, and the group's approval is an important factor in all their actions.

## 2. THE ORGANIZATIONAL STRUCTURE OF THE FIRMS

In the organizational hierarchy of large Swedish business firms one can generally distinguish six different groups of people: the members of the board of directors, the members of the top-management team, the middle management group, the clerical staff, the foremen and the workers. In some instances an individual person may belong to more than one group — the managing director and some other high executives may, for example, be members both of the board and the top-management team — in other cases it may be difficult to place him in any one of the particular groups, or two groups may overlap without a clear dividing line. There is, for example, no sharp demarcation between the middle management and the clerical staff in most companies. Nevertheless a distinction of these six different groups may be useful in a description of the organizational structure of the firms.

The size and composition of the board of directors varies somewhat as between different firms, but in most cases it consists of 5 to 8 people. The outside directors are generally in the majority. The boards of the large banks are larger, with up to 12 or 15 members. A study of the composition of the boards of 35 large industrial firms in 1943 showed that of a total of 225 seats, 35 were held by the managing directors of the firms, 17 by other top-management executives, 13 by previous managing directors who had retired, and 160 by people entirely outside the firm.[1] The majority of this latter group were managing directors or other high executives of other companies. The chairman of the board, who is elected by the board itself, generally belongs to this group. On the average the boards seem to meet 4 to 8 times a year, but there are boards which meet more frequently. The board of one of the firms connected with this study meets up to 30 times in a year, but that is exceptional. The main function of the boards is usually to consider major policies of the firms, their financial engagements and certain personnel problems relating to the top-management teams. Since the ownership of most big firms is divided amongst a large number of shareholders, most boards have a rather independent position.

What I have called the top-management team consists generally of the managing director and the sous-chefs and staff specialists working in most intimate contact with him A criterion of membership of this team may be that the person in question bears the title "director" or "assistant

---

[1] Sune Carlson, *op. cit.* p. 147.

director", that he takes part in the "directors' meetings", or that he sits at the "directors' tables" in the company canteen, but in many cases he is definitely a member even when these criteria are not fulfilled. It must be observed that in Sweden the title "director" does not imply that a person is member of the board of directors (*styrelsen*), and that the "directors' meeting" is the meeting of the top-management team and not of the board. In some cases it may be difficult to distinguish these executives who belong to the top-management team from the rest of the staff. There is not always a clear dividing line between them.

The size of the top-management team varies from 4 or 5 up to 15 or more. In some firms it meets in formal conferences practically every day, in others once a week, once a month or at even longer intervals. But there are daily contacts between most members of the team. Since the members generally have a similar background with respect to extraction, education and practical experience, their social status in the firm and in the local community tends to be fairly uniform. The differences relate mainly to age and other purely personal characteristics. The social position of the managing director is in some cases that of a *primus inter pares,* but in others it stands out as being considerably above that of the rest of the team. Some other members may also have a special standing either because they have the title and position of "deputy managing directors", or for other reasons, but this special standing relates more to their status in the firm than to their status in the community as a whole.

The middle management, the clerical staff, the foremen and the workers' groups are of less interest in this connection. The middle management group is the least homogeneous of the three. It is composed of people of different backgrounds and social standing and with different past careers and future prospects. Some of its members are university graduates and other people with a good training on their way up to the top-management group, others are faithful old servants who have reached their present positions in their firms after long and able service in some minor posts. In the industrial firms the foremen and workers groups stand out as clearly distinguishable units, although their social background and most of their social life is similar, the foremen nearly always being recruited from the workers. The clerical staff, which often enjoys some privileges with regard to working hours, length of vacations, canteen facilities, etc., which the foremen and workers do not have, is generally regarded as a separate group. With regard to their social position they may in most cases be classified as members of the middle management group. In the banks, the insurance companies and the department stores, there is much more difficulty in distinguishing between particular social groups below the top-management teams, and as a whole one must, of course, be careful in applying any kind of rigid classifications to the social groupings in a country with such a homogeneous population and such democratic traditions as Sweden.

## 3. THE RELATIONSHIPS BETWEEN THE FIRMS AND SOCIETY AT LARGE

There are some characteristic features of Swedish economic and political life that one must keep in mind, when one analyses the work of the business executives in the country. The small size of the Swedish economy is one of these and the high degree of centralized control over this economy is another. The freedom of activity of the individual business firm is curtailed not only by an increasing number of government regulations but by a huge variety of restrictions imposed by trade associations, trade unions, employers' federations and so on. Furthermore, with increased government control over business as one of the permanent topics in the political debate, and with improved news communication by press and radio, the activities of the individual firms and of the business in general have become of constant interest for the general public.

These developments have necessitated more consideration from the business executives than before regarding the implications for their respective firms of political and social changes, and have increased the need for various public relation activities, above all efficient representation of the firms towards government institutions, trade associations etc. For the chief executive it may be of much more importance that a trade negotiation which is going on between Sweden and a foreign country, or a negotiation between his industrial association and the Government Price Control Office, should turn out to the benefit of his firm, than that some purely commercial or organizational matter in the firm should be handled in a more efficient way. As we shall see later, considerations like these reflect to a large extent the patterns of his daily work.

*Chapter 4*

# WORKING TIME AND ITS DISTRIBUTION

How pleasant it is, at the end of the day,
No follies to have to repent;
But reflect on the past, and be able to say,
That my time has been properly spent.
*Jane Taylor*

## 1. REPORTING THE RESULTS

In presenting some of the results of our study in this and the following chapters, my main object will be to describe the analytical procedure employed. As mentioned before, our purpose was never to compute statistics of the "average" or "typical" behaviour of Swedish chief executives. The cases studied were far too few and far too heterogeneous for such a task. The results, consequently, were not averages but observational descriptions of individual cases and analytical comparisons between these cases. It is these observational descriptions which will first of all be reported here. I shall give examples of the type of statistics and diagrams employed, and I shall illustrate how these statistics and diagrams were used for the detection of deficiencies in the chief executives' administrative work. The data used in these illustrations will not always be taken from actual cases, but that is of minor importance in this connection.

The comparative analysis between the various cases showed that they had many characteristic features in common. Generally there were obvious reasons for these similarities, and the same features could often be noticed in other

Swedish firms of the same size and organizational structure. Some of these findings will also be presented here, but since this book is designed merely as a report on the actual study and not as a treatise on Swedish executive problems in general, the discussion of these points will be kept short.

## 2. PLACE OF WORK AND WORKING TIME

As has been mentioned in Chapter 2 the recording of the chief executives' working time outside the firm was attended by some difficulties. We had for example to leave it for the executives themselves to decide whether they regarded a particular occupation, such as reading trade journals or entertaining business associates in the evening, as work or not. Some general standards had, however, to be established regarding the treatment of such items as "working" lunches or dinners, travelling, or Sunday work in order to get comparability between the different cases. But I shall not deal with these problems here.

The data regarding the working time and the place of work were presented in diagrams of the type illustrated in figs. 3 and 4. The statistics shown in this diagram are

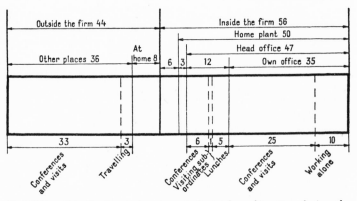

FIGURE 3. *Distribution in per cent of the total working time during the investigation period (24 days).*

hypothetical but they correspond fairly closely to some of the actual cases. Figure 3 illustrates the percentage distribution of the chief executive's total working time during the weekdays in the investigation period. At the top of the figure the time distribution relates to the various places of work according to the classification system mentioned in Chapter 2 (p. 42). These statistics are supplemented by figures for various types of occupations such as "conferences", "travelling" or "working alone". In fig. 4 the time distribution given relates to the weekdays — except Saturdays — which the chief executive spent at the head office. Thus, in this case we have excluded the days when the chief executive did not visit the office at all, as well as Saturdays, when the office hours generally end at lunch. What we have tried to compute is the time distribution during a "normal" day at the office, and for that purpose we have also included figures of the average number of minutes for the various occupations. In the example given the average total working time is 10 hours. The median figure in the study was around 9 ¾ hours, and the individual figures varied between 8 ½ and 11 ½ hours.

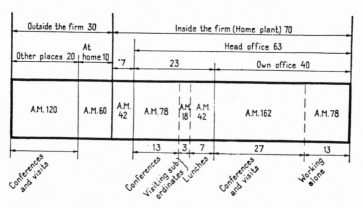

FIGURE 4. *Distribution in per cent of the working time during the weekdays — except saturdays — when the executive was at the head office (18 days).*

The analysis of the chief executive's working time and its distribution revealed in the individual cases examples of some administrative deficiencies which may be of general interest. Among these were problems connected with

the activities outside the firm;
the lack of time for inspecting and visiting works and offices;
the lack of time for reading and contemplation; and
the excessive nature of the total working load.

I shall comment on some of our findings regarding each of these groups of problems.

## 3. ACTIVITIES OUTSIDE THE FIRM

The amount of time Swedish chief executives have to spend outside their own firms in conferences and meetings with government authorities, trade associations, employers' federations etc. must be seen against the background of the particular features of the Swedish economy which I have indicated in Chapter 3. If we include "working" lunches and dinners outside the firm but exclude the time spent on travelling, or on work at home, the median for the time spent on work outside the firm represented 32 % of the total working time. In order to get the total time occupied in connection with these outside activities, we should add the time taken up by preparation for the various meetings. Nevertheless we had selected the investigation period for some of the members with special consideration to the fact that they would not be away too much while the study was going on. There were considerable differences regarding the distribution of the outside work between the chief executives of firms in Stockholm and those of firms in the country. While the former spent some time on outside meetings almost every day, the latter could concentrate this activity into the days when they were in the capital. While at home they were relatively undisturbed by outside activities.

In order to get a more reliable picture of this part of the chief executives' work we collected supplementary information regarding the number of formal conferences and meetings outside the firms they had attended during the last year together with the total time they had been away from their head offices during the same period. These data regarding outside conferences and meetings verified the difference mentioned above between the executives in Stockholm and those in the provinces. The total number of outside conferences attended by the former is considerably higher. The amount of time spent outside the firm can be measured in different ways. We decided to add together all absences lasting at least a quarter of a day, and obtained in this way individual figures varying between 64 and 165 days in the year. In some cases a remarkably high "absentee figure" was explained by unusually long business tours to foreign countries, but in others they related merely to what may be regarded as quite normal activities in the daily life of a managing director.

When the head of a business firm has to spend up to half his working time outside his headquarters the top-management of the firm must generally be organized in a different way from what would be appropriate if he could be at home most of the time. But this is not always done. Most chief executives were trained for their present jobs at a time when the outside activities of a managing director were less important than today, and they often regard these activities not as a normal part of their job but as an extra burden, which they wishfully think of as being of a temporary nature. Since they hope that life will return to "normal" times soon again, they do not plan their work in

[65]

such a way as they would if they regarded the present external activities as permanent.

This attitude of "I hope we shall soon return to normal times" has another consequence. As members of the boards of trade associations, employers' federations and so on, the chief executives seldom take the necessary initiative regarding the rationalization of these associations. As a consequence of general political and economic developments these institutions have grown in size and complexity, and their working organization is not as a rule adjusted to their present activities and work loads. The liaison between these institutions and the individual firms is seldom efficiently organized. All this hampers the work of the chief executive, who has to spend more time at various meetings than would be necessary if the activities of the respective institutions were better organized.

There were chief executives in our study who had organized the management of their firms in such a manner that they could be away a large part of their working time without any major difficulties arising. The management of these firms was characterized by a far-reaching decentralization of authority and responsibility, and by the fact that a definite person or a committee of persons was appointed to deputize permanently for the managing director when he was away. In other firms the chief executive might be absent from the office much less, and nevertheless there were definite signs of a "vacuum" in the top-management. There was irritation among subordinates because of the lack of contact with the chief executive and because of the delays in decision-making. I shall return to some of these questions later on, and shall only comment on one aspect of the problem here: the question of deputies for the chief executives.

In banks and department stores, where the success of the business greatly depends on the top-management's ability to take quick decisions, the deputy problem is generally solved in a satisfactory way. They have been forced to find a solution. But when this pressure is absent a chief executive can find many reasons for not doing anything about the problem or for postponing its solution until another time. The existence of a deputy managing director gives rise to a multitude of communication and subordination problems and it has also a bearing on the selection of future chief executives. Nevertheless, in view both of the amount of time the chief executive has to spend outside the firm, and of the risk involved in not having anybody to take charge of the firm in case he suddenly becomes ill or dies, a definite solution of the deputy problem is highly desirable in any firm above a certain size and complexity. Fayol's old recommendation that everybody in an organization should have a deputy well trained to step into his shoes when necessary also holds true at the very top of the organization.

The top-management problems connected with the chief executive's outside work were generally not the same in the Stockholm firms as the provincial firms. As was mentioned before, the Stockholm executives spent some part of their time outside almost every day, while the chief executives of the provincial firms could generally concentrate their outside activities into the days when they were in Stockholm. In the former case the problems were not so obvious, but they existed nevertheless. The main difficulty was to organize the executive work in such a way that the managing director could leave the firm at short notice and stay away for varying periods without interrupting the daily running of the firm. Some of the executives studied were, for example, members of committees in which representatives from the industry collaborated with cabinet ministers on some urgent economic problems, and generally these committees had to meet at very short notice. Since in other cases also they could not tell beforehand exactly when and how long they would have to be away, the planning of their appointments and other engagements became difficult. A common cause of irritation was the mere fact that the outside engagements of the chief executive were not or could not be notified to the proper persons beforehand. A sous-chef or a department head who wanted to see his superior on an urgent matter often found to his surprise that the latter was away and that it was uncertain when he would be back. It was not surprising that under such circumstances the queue waiting at the door tended to be rather long when the chief executive returned, and the existence of this queue was another cause for complaint.

The provincial executives had another problem. They generally knew beforehand when they had to be away and could notify their subordinates accordingly, but they had to stay away for longer periods. They had either to delegate all necessary powers of decision to their sous-chefs during the periods of absence or to keep in daily contact with their home offices by mail and telephone. There were successful examples of both methods among the cases studied.

With all the difficulties and personal discomfort associated with the chief executives' increasing outside activities, this work has had at least one positive effect: it has taught the subordinates to take decisions by themselves and not to trouble the chief executives unnecessarily.

### 4. INSPECTION TOURS AND VISITS TO WORKS AND OFFICES

As might be expected, the main part of the chief executives' working time inside their firms was taken up by visitors and conferences of various kinds. I shall, however, postpone the discussion of this part of their work to the next two chapters, where I shall deal with the general question of contacts and communication. Here I propose to take up another aspect of their work: their inspection tours to plants and offices and their visits to subordinates outside the executive office.

In fig. 3 the time spent on inspection tours and visits is obtained by adding the items

| | | |
|---|---|---|
| visits | to plants outside the home plant | 6 % |
| ,, | to home plant outside the head office | 3 % |
| ,, | to subordinates in the head office | 1 % |
| | total | 10 % |

Fig. 4, which relates to the "normal" working days at the head office, contains the figures

| | | |
|---|---|---|
| visits | to home plant outside the head office | 7 % |
| ,, | to subordinates in the head office | 3 % |
| | total | 10 % |

which corresponds to an average inspection and visit time of $(42+18)$ 60 minutes a day. But these figures are given only in order to demonstrate the method of analysis and presentation. They are not typical.

The actual amount of time spent on inspection tours and visits varied considerably as between the individual executives. To some extent the variations could be explained by differences in structure among the individual firms. The need for personal inspection tours by the chief executive is not the same in a bank or an insurance company as in an industrial firm or a department store, and it varies also with the geographical concentration or dispersion of the firm's premises. But irrespective of these differences the study indicated on this point considerable variations in the working methods as between the individual executives.

From conversations. and interviews it became clear that

[69]

the chief executives themselves regarded personal inspection tours in plants and offices as a most important duty. There was also a general regret that this task could not be attended to sufficiently because of lack of time. Nevertheless most executives seemed to be mistaken as to the amount of inspection work they actually did. Wishful thinking led them to believe that things were not so bad as they really were. To the question: "How often do you make inspection tours in the plant?" we frequently got answers like "once a fortnight" or "once every three weeks" in spite of the fact that the executive in question had not been down in the plant for several months. He knew, of course, that he had not made any inspection tour the last month, but there was a special reason for that; and not the month before either, but that was also because of something extraordinary. He had, however, forgotten that it was a very long time ago since he really had the chance to fulfil his wish to make regular inspection tours.

Although the chief executive of a large organization has to rely on statistical reports and memoranda for most of his information, these reports and memoranda do not generally cover all aspects of the firm's activities. Particularly with regard to such matters as discipline, working conditions, cleanliness etc. a personal inspection tour reveals so much more than mere report reading can do. During an inspection tour the executive also has a chance to come in contact with subordinates whom he otherwise would not meet, and he can observe these subordinates in their normal working environment. When a subordinate has to visit the chief executive in the head office, it is only too probable that this visit will have the character of a dress rehearsal — his behaviour will not be so natural as it is when he is in his own working place.

In the study, however, we found individual executives

who spent a considerable time out in plants and offices, but they had made their inspection tours an integratal part of their daily routine. There is a tendency for business executives to become slaves to their appointment diaries — they get a kind of "diary complex". One can seldom see two business executives talking together without their diaries in their hands, and they feel rather lost unless they know that they have these diaries within easy reach. When they start their working day they will look up what they have to do, and whatever is in the diary they will fulfil punctually and efficiently. If one wants to be sure of getting something done by this group of people, one has to see to that it gets into their diaries. One should never ask a busy executive to promise to do something e. g. "next week" or even "next Friday". Such vague requests do not get entered into his appointment diary. No, one has to state a specific time, say, Friday 4.15 p.m., then it will be put down and in due course done. The more exactly the time is specified, the more certain it will be that the task will be attended to. The trouble is, however, that sometimes what is entered in the appointment diary is not what is of most importance for the chief executive but what is important to other people. If such tasks as inspection tours and visits of subordinates in their offices are to have the same chance of being done as board meetings or lunches with business associates they must have a definite place in the executive's normal working routine.

### 5. TIME FOR READING AND CONTEMPLATION

The length of time during which the chief executives could work in their offices undisturbed by visitors varied considerably as between the individual persons. For some of them this time amounted to less than half an hour during a "normal" weekday, for others it was as much as an hour or an hour and a half. Indeed, in one extreme case the average time for "working alone" reached three hours a day, but that was explained by the fact that the executive in question went to the office in the mornings two hours before everyone else.

These figures for the average daily time for "working

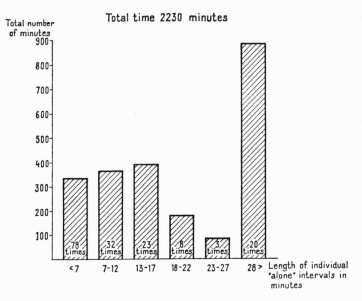

FIGURE 5. *The distribution of the total time during which the chief executive worked alone in his office undisturbed by visitors.*

alone" are not, however, so illuminating as the statistics of how this time is distributed in intervals of different length. Examples of such distributions, taken from one of the actual cases studied, are given in figs. 5 and 6. They relate to a chief executive who during a "normal" weekday had an average total time for "working alone" in his office of as much as 1 hour and 28 minutes. In all he was undisturbed *by visitors* 2230 minutes during the investigation period, but as can be seen from fig. 5 this time was mainly composed of short "alone" intervals with an average length of 10 or 15 minutes. (The arithmetic mean was in fact 14 minutes.) If one considers that many of these intervals were split up by telephone calls, the actual situation with regard to time for undisturbed work is still less favourable. As is shown in fig. 6, during the investigation period the exe-

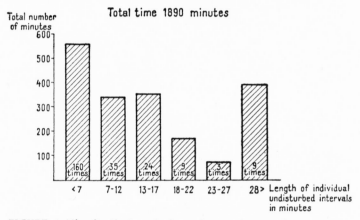

FIGURE 6. *The distribution of the total time during which the chief executive worked alone in his office undisturbed by visitors and telephone calls.*

cutive in question had a total time undisturbed *by visitors and telephone calls* of 1890 minutes, but nearly half of this time related to short "alone" intervals of up to around 10 minutes. (The arithmetic mean was 8 minutes.) Only 12 times in 35 days did the chief executive work undisturbed in his office during intervals of 23 minutes or more.

"Alone" intervals of 5 or 10 minutes are, of course, not only of little value for working purposes, but are also unsatisfactory as rest intervals. It is characteristic that but few if any of the executives had any idea that they spent up to an hour or an hour and a half "alone" during the day. All they knew was that they had scarcely had time to start on a new task or to sit down and light a cigarette before they

[73]

were interrupted by a visitor or a telephone call. It is only when the "alone" interval is of a certain minimum length that it can be utilized efficiently. In order to get more time for those tasks which demand concentration and peace of mind most executives must organize their working day in a different way from what they do today. First of all, they must delegate much more of their detail work to their subordinates. Individual cases studied showed that a lot can be done in the right direction merely by the help of secretaries and telephone operators who are trained to protect the chief executives against unnecessary disturbances, by the introduction of fixed reception hours for certain types of visitors or telephone calls and by various types of instructions to the subordinates. But it is no easy task, and in order to succeed the chief executive must secure the loyal help of everybody in the organization whom he has to deal with regularly.

Since the majority of the chief executives never had enough time undisturbed by visitors and telephone calls while at their offices, they had to bring a considerable amount of work home with them. An average working time at home of one hour and a half per day was a normal figure. The main part of the work at home consisted of reading of trade journals and memoranda of various kinds and of reviewing statistical reports. Some executives mentioned that they also had to do all dictation and writing which needed real concentration at home, and one used his home also for the more important conferences with people both from the firm and from outside. Provided that the chief executive would not be more disturbed in his office than in his home, it seems that he would do most of this work much more efficiently in his office, where he has access to all the necessary documents and information.

## 6. TOTAL WORKING LOAD

Trough we had no way of measuring quantitatively the working loads of the chief executives, the study of their total working time and of the type of their work indicated that in most cases this working load was excessively heavy. As was mentioned above their average total working time during "normal" weekdays varied between 8 $\frac{1}{2}$ and 11 $\frac{1}{2}$ hours, and to this should be added work at home during weekends. The effect of this excessive working load is felt both by the executives themselves and by their organizations. With one exception all the executives we interviewed testified that in the long run they could not continue with their present amount of work, and all the private secretaries without exception complained about the excessive working load of their chiefs.

For the chief executives themselves this excessive working load has many unpleasant effects. It means that their opportunities to be with their families or to see their private friends are severely curtailed, and it entails travelling in night trains and evenings and weekends spent away from home. In some cases it also causes a certain intellectual isolation. It is usually only on vacations and during some of their tours to foreign countries that the chief executives can get away from the constant pressure of work. They seldom have time to read anything but technical and economic literature or to go to a theatre or a concert. One of the executives said in an interview that he had had to sacrifice all his literary interests and his chances to see his personal friends in order to keep up with his work, and another testified that he had not had time to see any of his private friends during the last five years. These may be exceptional cases, but there was no one who did not complain of insufficient time for reading and other cultural activities, for sport and for rest.

The negative effects of these circumstances are felt, however, not only by the chief executives themselves but also by their firms. It seems to me that there is a definite need at the present time for industrial leaders with a wide knowledge of current social and cultural affairs, and it is impossible to acquire and maintain such a knowledge if one must spend all one's free time reading technical literature and business reports. There is also another aspect of this problem. It is only natural that the chief executive's way of working should become the standard for his subordinates. Instead of considering work on overtime as something exceptional the people around the chief executive are led to regard it as the rule, and instead of widening their general cultural education they specialize themselves more and more in their own limited trades. Indeed, there are firms where the reading even of trade journals and more general business reports is not regarded as legitimate work. That under such circumstances industry has difficulty in recruiting leaders is not so difficult to understand.

The study showed, however, that there existed noticeable exceptions from the conditions described here. It is possible to lighten the working load of the chief executives. But that is a question which I shall return to after the discussion of some of the other aspects of the chief executive's work.

# Chapter 5

# PROBLEMS OF COMMUNICATION

It has long been an axiom of mine that the little things
are infinitely the most important.

*Sherlock Holmes*

## 1. THE ORGANIZATIONAL STRUCTURE

In our study of the chief executives' communications with
other people we have made a distinction between direct
and indirect contacts. The former included personal observations, e. g. during an inspection tour in a plant, conversations person to person, telephone calls and conferences. The
indirect contacts included communication via other persons
such as secretaries or staff assistants, and communication by
means of reports, memoranda, letters and other kinds of
paper. The contacts were related both to people inside the
organization and to people from the outside.

For the study of the chief executives' contacts inside their
organizations it was necessary to have some knowledge of
the local and social environment in which the chief executives worked. We had to know something about (a) their
physical environment, the location and size of the various
operational units, the lay-outs of the head offices etc., (b)
the formal organizational structures of their firms, and (c)
the types of social relations existing between the people in
the executives' immediate surroundings. While there is
little to be said about the material we collected regarding
the physical environments, the data relating to the formal

and informal organizational structures of the firms may deserve a few comments.

In our study of the formal organizations of the firms the main task was to prepare up-to-date organization charts of the type shown in fig. 7.[1] The purpose of these charts was to illustrate the formal lines of communication between the chief executives and their various subordinates. Supplementary information was collected regarding the existence of regular committees and conferences in which the chief executives used to take part, with data regarding the composition of these committees and conferences and the type and frequency of their meetings. Since our investigation was limited to firms whose organization problems we had already studied and discussed fairly intensively in other connections, most of the data needed were easy to get. Still, to portray a living organization in a simple chart is always difficult. In actual practice the lines of communication between the various persons involved do not always follow a logical pattern, and the formal status of a particular person is in many cases obscure. The present state of an organization can often be understood only after a study of its history. It is not the product of a definite plan, but has grown up through an evolutionary process. New persons have been added from time to time and others have been shifted around or moved to meet specific needs on the basis of expediency, and in many instances it is the organization that has been adapted to the particular persons and not the other way around.

There are, however, many social patterns and relationships in a firm which do not appear in a formal organization chart. There are cliques of people who regard themselves as belonging together and as superior or inferior to other cliques, and there are various kinds of groups who may or may not keep in social contact with other groups. In Chapter

---

[1] Facing page 80.

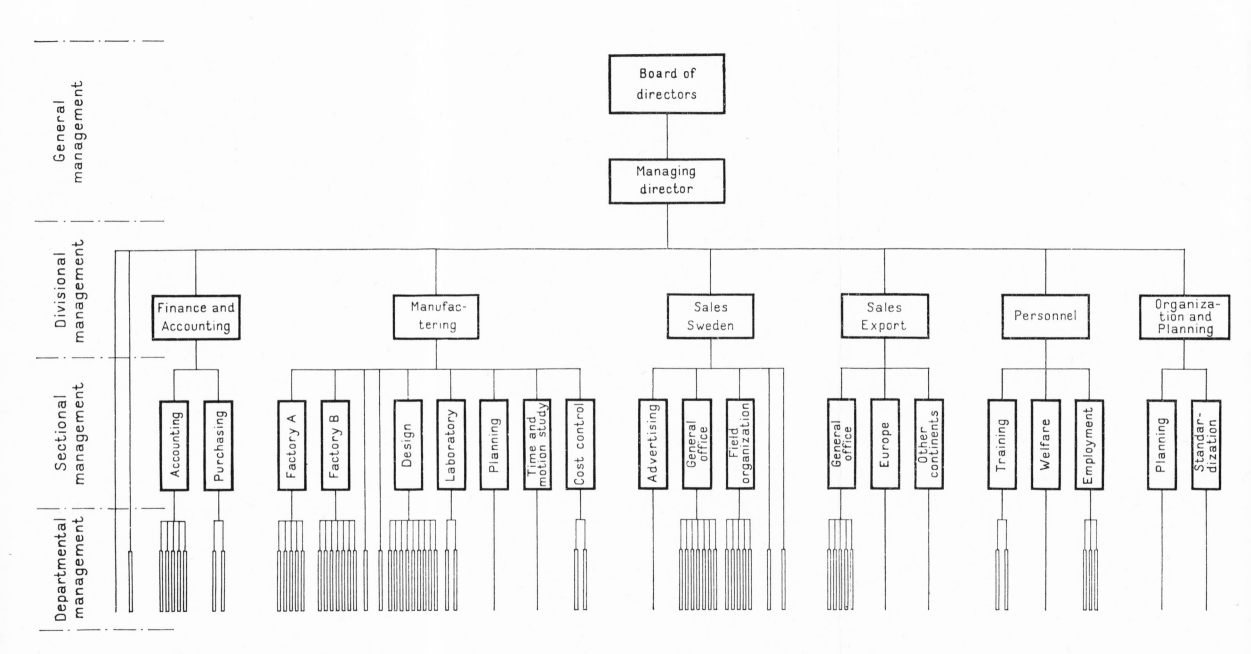

FIGURE 7. *Organization chart illustrating the formal lines of communi-cation between the chief executive and his various subordinates.*

3 I have sketched some major groups who can generally be found in the social organization of large Swedish business firms. But other groups also exist. A knowledge of how this informal organizational structure is built up and is functioning is a pre-requisite for the understanding of the actual working of the lines of communication between the chief executive and the members of his organization.

Now it is much more difficult to understand and describe the informal organizational structure than the formal one. While the duties and formal position of a member of an organization can generally be defined in fairly exact terms, his group affiliation, informal status or social contact patterns can only be apprehended indirectly after a study of various symbols. I shall illustrate this by an example.

In the Swedish language we have two words for the English word you: *Du* and *Ni*. *Du,* which corresponds to the German *du* or the French *tu* and *toi,* is informal and *Ni,* which corresponds to the German *Sie* and the French *vous,* is formal. *Du* is used not only between family members and personal friends but also between acquaintances, colleagues, business associates etc. who regard themselves as members of the same group. Its usage is similar to the usage of Christian names in Great Britain or America. Thus, by merely observing which persons in an organization call each other *Du* or *Ni* we may get some indication of the social grouping. An example of this is shown in figure 8. The diagram relates to a small manufacturing firm, and it is based on data which were collected by one of my students for a seminar paper a few years ago. In the formal organization of the firm the managing director had next to him three section heads: a merchandising manager, an office manager and a works manager, and next to these managers there were respectively three, four and five subordinates in supervisory position. All these people worked in the same place. In order to describe the social groupings, observations were made (1) regarding their sex, age and income and (2) regarding the usage of *Du* or *Ni* as indicated above. The result is shown in fig. 8. The conclusions which can be drawn from an analysis of this diagram may perhaps be summarized in the following way: If we regard the usage of the word *Du* as an indicator of group affiliation

(a) this affiliation was total among the supervisors inside each individual section,

(b) and between the supervisors in the merchandizing and office sections, while the supervisors in the works section were isolated from the rest;

(c) another group seems to have been formed by the managing director and the merchandising and office managers, who all belonged to the same age and income groups, and the head of the sales department, while the works manager was left outside in spite of his age and income status;

(d) the importance of the income factor was illustrated also by the social position of the heads of the statistical and the models departments.

It must be noticed, however, that a diagram of the type shown in fig. 8 does not describe the informal organization of a firm in the same way as fig. 7, for example, describes a formal organization. It merely illustrates certain symbols which we use as indicators of the social status patterns and the informal grouping we are trying to fathom. These symbols may be appropriate or not, but they are merely symbols. Besides the characteristics for group status and social relation patterns mentioned,

sex
age
income and
usage of *Du* or *Ni*

the following have been found most useful:

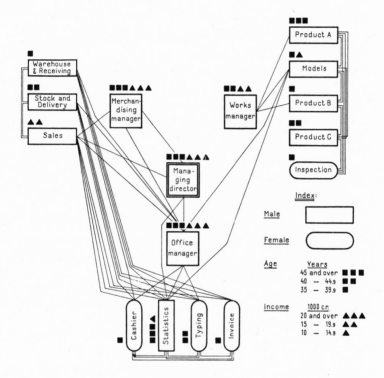

*FIGURE 8. Chart indicating group affiliation and group status in a small manufacturing firm.*

Those executives and supervisors in the organization who address one another by the informal *Du* are connected by lines.

usage of titles (which is very important in Sweden, where
no one likes to be plain "Mister"),
formal education,
time in office,
type and situation of office room, and
place and company for lunch.

As a complement to the formal organization chart this
information was of great help for the understanding of
"who is who" in the organization, and of what a particular executive contact actually "meant".


## 2.  THE CONTACT CHARTS

The data collected regarding the chief executives' contacts with various persons and institutions during the
observation period were presented in special contact charts
of the type shown in figures 9 (facing p. 88) and 10 (facing
p. 96). Figure 9 illustrates the contacts between the chief
executive and his subordinates made in internal committee
meetings and fig. 10 his other contacts. But since we did
not succeed in recording all the personal contacts which the
executive had outside his office, e. g. when walking through
a plant or an office, the data regarding his internal personal
contacts illustrated in this latter type of diagram were
never complete. The cases illustrated in the two contact
charts in fig. 9 and 10, which should be studied in connection with the organization chart in fig. 7, are hypothetical,
but most of their traits are in line with cases actually
studied.

As was mentioned in Chapter 2 the chief executives' outside contacts were classified in 11 different classes. In fig.
10 I have included only 10 — the classes, "Private visitors"
and "Others" forming only one class. For every class there
are two bars indicating the number of times (the figures at

the top of the bar) and the length of time (the length of the bar) the chief executive has been in personal contact with representatives of the class. If the bar is placed to the left, it indicates that the meeting has taken place within the firm; if it is placed to the right, that the meeting was outside the firm. A shaded bar means that the visitor or the chief executive has been accompanied by someone else, a black bar that the chief executive has been alone with the person in question. The letter T together with a figure shows the number of telephone calls the chief executive has had with, and the letter L together with a figure the number of letters he has written to, representatives of the class. Thus, the contact chart indicates that the chief executive in question has had 9 personal contacts and 4 telephone calls with, and has written 7 letters to, "Official authorities". Of the personal contacts one took place in the executive's own office. During this visit, which lasted 60 minutes, another member of the organization was present. Of the 8 contacts taking place outside the firm, which lasted 910 minutes altogether, the executive was accompanied by various subordinates during 6 contacts which lasted 610 minutes.

The chief executive's contacts with his own subordinates are illustrated in a similar way. As regards the contacts made during internal committee meetings, which are recorded in fig. 9, data are also given regarding the number of meetings in each particular committee and the total duration of these meetings.

The analysis of these contact charts was perhaps the most interesting and important part of our whole study. It was supplemented by a study of other material, obtained by interviews and by other means.[1] This latter study was of particular importance for a correction of the contact pictures we got from the charts, which in some respects were strongly influenced by seasonal variations.

[1] See pp. 49—50.

## 3. OUTSIDE CONTACTS

As mentioned in the last chapter, we had selected the investigation period for some of the members with special consideration to the fact that they would not be away too much while the study was going on. It is therefore probable that the contact charts did not give a representative picture of the chief executives' outside contacts. Some of these contacts have a definite seasonal pattern. For example the annual or bi-annual meetings of trade associations, chambers of commerce and employers' federations generally take place in the spring and late autumn, and the customers in foreign countries visit generally the export firms during the summer. In order to get a more reliable picture of the outside contacts we supplemented the communication study by collecting data regarding the associations, boards and outside committees, of which the chief executives were regular members, the number of meetings these various institutions had had during the last 12 months and the number of meetings attended by the chief executives.

Although the contact pattern varied considerably as between the different executives they had some characteristic features in common. One of the most noticeable of these was the limited use of letters as a means of communication. There were chief executives who signed not more than one or two letters a week, and the maximum was two or three letters a day. The picture of the chief executive as a man who is busy dictating and signing letters was not borne out by any of our studies.[1]

---

[1] According to the study of 12 German executives mentioned in Chapter 1, these persons spent on the average 2 hours a day dictating and ½ hour a day signing letters! (Cf. "Die tägliche Arbeitsleistung der Direktoren", *op. cit.* pp. 608—611.) The study of 21 city managers, mentioned by Nolting, shows, that these executives spent on the average one hour a day in "handling correspondence" (*cf.* O. F. Nolting, *Management Methods in City Government, op. cit.* p. 1).

As regards the place for the personal meetings between the chief executive and the people from outside, this varied in the different categories. The meetings with representatives of official authorities, trade associations and employers' federations generally took place outside the firms. The most common outside visitors to the executives' own offices were the representatives of scientific institutions, customers, suppliers and other firms with which the chief executives had contacts. One may perhaps observe a certain difference as between chief executives in Swedish banks and in other firms, which is rather interesting. The former category is not expected to pay so many visits to other firms. They are generally visited.

The distribution of the outside contacts among different categories of people varied a great deal from one executive to another. A common feature was the low frequency of their contacts with customers and suppliers. While these contacts were generally delegated to other persons in the organizations according to a rational plan, there seemed to be no corresponding delegation with regard to the contacts which related to what may be called the firms' non-commercial activities, e. g. the representation of the firm vis-à-vis government offices, trade associations and professional and welfare institutions. Many contacts that today are handled by the chief executive himself could probably be taken care of just as efficiently by someone else in the organization. The lack of initiative in this respect is connected with the fact, mentioned above, that most executives wishfully hope that many of these activities will prove to be of a temporary nature. In order to get more direct knowledge of these problems the members of the group are at present engaged in a more extensive study of the non-commercial relations between the firms and the community at large.

The picture is entirely different with regard to the

contacts the chief executives have with firms in which they are board members. The communication with these firms is regarded as most important and interesting. It gives an insight into the management problems of other industries and is a valuable complement to the chief executive's own experience.

## 4. INTERNAL COMMITTEES

If we include the board of directors among the internal committees of the firm, this committee is, at least in Sweden, rather different in its character and working methods from the other internal committees. I have mentioned in Chapter 3 that the boards of directors in large Swedish companies generally consist of 5 to 8 persons, of whom the majority are from outside. The boards seem to meet on the average 4 to 8 times a year, but there are boards which meet more frequently. Two of the firms investigated in this study had board meetings regularly once a month, and one firm once a fortnight. Some of the chief executives had, however, regular informal contacts with one or several board members between the formal meetings. Although most of the executives spent considerable time in preparing the agenda for the board meetings, none of them regarded the communication with the board and its individual members as a particularly time-consumming or difficult task.

If we pass on to the other internal committees, we shall find that these committees often represent an important means for the chief executives to keep in regular contact with their subordinates. A comparison of the two contact charts in fig. 9 and 10 shows that the chief executive's committee contacts are both more systematic and more varying with regard to the type of people he meets than his other personal contacts inside the organization. This observation was true for most of the executives. Of particular importance as contact means for the chief executives are the labour-management committees and the conferences with the foremen and the sales staff. In these committees he gets a chance to meet representatives of those classes of subordinates who work outside his ordinary surroundings and with whom he has little chance to keep in contact otherwise. But the other committees are also of great value for the chief executive, when he wants to keep himself informed about what is going on in his firm, or when he wants to get ideas or information across to other people.

In the case illustrated in fig. 9 the chief executive is shown to have attended, during the investigation period, 5 different committees with in all 9 meetings. Of the 9 Swedish executives actually studied the majority attended regularly the meetings of at least 4 different types of committees and conferences. But it is difficult to draw a line between these formal committees and conferences and the *ad hoc* meetings which the executives attended. For example, the total number of internal committee meetings in which one executive took part during a year was said to be about a dozen, while the corresponding figure for another was 350—400, but these figures do not tell us very much. Everything depends on how one defines the term "committee meeting".

If one considers the amount of time which is spent in committee sessions not only by some of these chief executives themselves but also by the members of their staff, the planning and running of the committee work stands out as one of the most important executive tasks. As it is now, this committee work is often impaired by unnecessary shortcomings. Among our findings in this connection, I may mention

a tendency to let the number of members in a committee

increase without considering the effect on the working efficiency,

a difficulty in limiting the time of the individual sessions,

a lack of coordination between committee proceedings and other means of internal communication such as reports and memoranda,

a growing difficulty in following up decisions taken in committee sessions when these are attended by an increasing number of people and when they grow in frequency and duration, and

a tendency to use committees composed of already overworked people as a substitute for staff assistants for the handling of matters which need full-time attention.

But as these are problems related more to top-management in general than to the working methods of the chief executives, I shall not enter into a discussion of them here.

## 5. OTHER CONTACTS WITH SUBORDINATES

Though the internal committees represented an important means for some of the chief executives with regard to their personal contacts with subordinates, the *ad hoc* meetings were generally of still greater significance both with regard to their frequency and their consumption of time. We have seen in the last chapter that when the chief executive was in his office, there were but short intervals when he was not disturbed by telephone calls and visitors. The vast majority of these visits were from people inside the organization. I shall, however, postpone the analysis of this particular kind of internal contact to the next chapter.

There were also other means for the chief executives to keep in direct contact with their subordinates. I have mentioned earlier that there were executives who spent a considerable time out in plants and offices, where they came in contact with many subordinates whom they would not meet otherwise, but I observed also that this was more the exception than the rule. Lunches and dinners were also used as means of keeping in contact with special groups of subordinates. Most of the chief executives had lunch almost daily either with some of their immediate subordinates or with other people associated with their business, and they were present at dinners and other kinds of personnel gatherings about once a month. Some of them entertained various groups of subordinates at dinner in their own homes at regular intervals. As a whole these kinds of informal social contacts were regarded as an important and efficient complement to the more formal channels of communication between the chief executives and the members of their staff.

## 6. WRITTEN COMMUNICATIONS

The larger the organization is, the more important the written communications become for the chief executive in the contacts with his subordinates. Like other communication media written communications can be used in two directions. Letters, memoranda and policy statements flow down the line from the executive office and records and reports flow up. In our study we collected data regarding all the letters to subordinates signed by the chief executive during the investigation period, and all the records and reports that he recieved. The latter part of the investigation extended over one full year and covered the number, the size and the main contents of all written material of a periodic nature. Like the other parts of the study this was supplemented by interview data.

The vast majority of written communications used by the chief executives were of the incoming kind. It was relatively seldom that they used written communication media when they themselves had to convey anything to their subordinates. Letters, memoranda, policy statements etc. were mainly

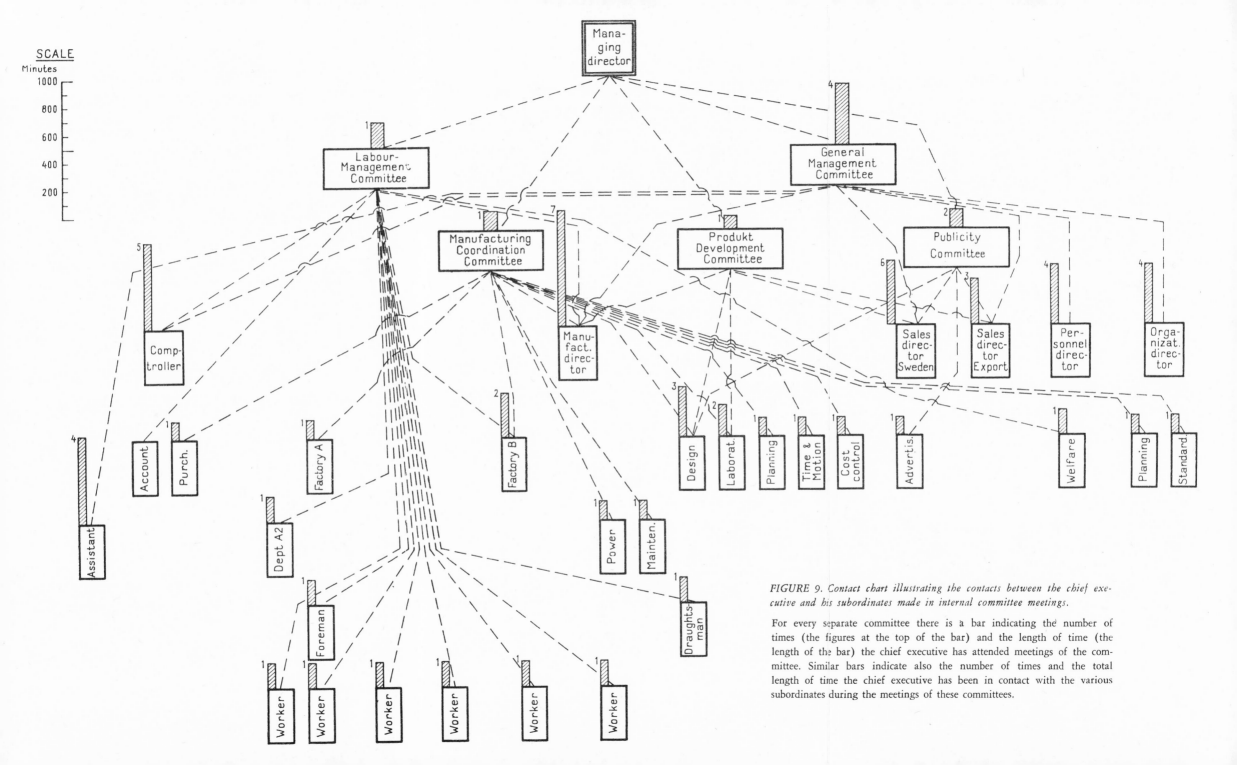

FIGURE 9. *Contact chart illustrating the contacts between the chief executive and his subordinates made in internal committee meetings.*

For every separate committee there is a bar indicating the number of times (the figures at the top of the bar) and the length of time (the length of the bar) the chief executive has attended meetings of the committee. Similar bars indicate also the number of times and the total length of time the chief executive has been in contact with the various subordinates during the meetings of these committees.

produced at other levels of the organizations. Some executives occasionally wrote letters to subordinates, or they wrote editorials or articles in the company magazine in order to get into touch with the rank and file in their organizations, but as a whole their own writing was mainly related to their outside contacts.

The way in which internal records and reports were used as a means of information varied greatly as between the different executives. These variations related both to the contents and type of the records and reports and to their size and frequency. There were executives who received only a hundred or a few hundred pages of regular reports in the course of a year, while the corresponding figure for other executives was several thousand. The differences could partly be explained by the character and organizational structure of their firms, by they were also related to purely personal factors. The desire and capacity to consume reports seems to vary considerably from person to person.

On the whole the system of internal reports seemed to work well in the firms studied. The only complaint heard from some of the chief executives was that the number or size of the reports had a tendency to grow more and more, and that it had become impossible to read them all. One of them said that he would like to get only those statistics which showed deviations from the normal and not a lot of figures which only showed that everything was as it should be.

If one takes into consideration the limited time a chief executive has for undisturbed reading, one must indeed ask if all the internal records and reports he receives are really necessary. There are other things besides reports to be read. Of course, there are many reports which are never read, and never will be, but these reports nevertheless form a part of that paper ballast on the executive's desk or in his briefcase, which is the cause of so much mental agony. The rationalization of the chief executives' paper work, and the better coordination of this work with their other activities constitute an important means for lessening their work load and saving their time.

## 7. PROBLEMS OF COMMUNICATION TECHNIQUE

The technique of communication used by the chief executive in his contacts with other persons varies a great deal as between the different categories of people he has contact with. There are certain people with whom he must have frequent direct and indirect contacts. To this group belong such categories as the firm's banking connections, the employers' federations and certain important government institutions. The means of communication used in these contacts are mainly conferences and visits paid by the chief executive to the persons in question, but the use of the telephone and of memoranda and reports is also frequent. Inside the firm the chief executive has frequent contacts with his sous-chefs and with some staff assistants. Often some of the members of the board of directors are included in this group. The means of communication are the same as above, with the difference that the person-to-person conversations generally take place in the chief executive's own office.

There are other categories of people with whom the chief executive's contacts are mainly indirect. His communication with customers and suppliers and with some trade associations and some official authorities is mainly carried on by means of letters, memoranda and reports, although these means are supplemented by telephone calls and by occasional conferences and personal conversations. Inside the firm most of the subordinates dealt with are contacted by the same means.

Several comments have already been made regarding the

technique of communication and I shall make some more in the next chapter. Here I shall only take up two particular aspects of this technique, the chief executive's reception of visitors and his use of the telephone.

As has been mentioned earlier we supplemented the data on the communication technique obtained in the observational study by interviews with the private secretaries, the telephone exchange operators and the chief executives themselves. We also made direct observations regarding such matters as the layout of the head offices and the working of the internal communication system. There is no doubt that these local amenities and organizational arrangements have a great influence on the chief executives in their daily work. Like all other craftsmen they are dependent on their working environment. The rearrangement of the office layout in such a way that no one can enter or leave the chief executive's room without passing the room of his private secretary, the introduction of red stop lights at the door, or new instructions to the telephone exchange operator regarding the way to sift incoming telephone calls will have an immediate effect on the executive's behaviour patterns. Indeed, it is mainly by the use of such means that his behaviour can be changed. An executive who knows that he talks too much on the telephone or spends too much time with visitors will have very little chance to change his habits so long as the telephone calls and the visitors are not screened for him.

With the notable exception of two or three cases it seemed as if the chief executives did not make full use of their private secretaries and personal assistants in the handling of visitors. If these people are to be able to save the executive's time by taking care of some of the visitors themselves or by referring them to other members of the organization, they must, of course, have a thorough knowledge of how the organization works. In addition they must have instructions to ask not only for the names of the visitors but also for the reasons for their visits. With such a knowledge at their disposal they are also in a much better position to prepare in advance the documents and notes, which the chief executive is going to need during the actual visits. The few cases where the reception of visitors was arranged in this manner indicated that a considerable saving of executive time can be achieved by an able and properly trained private secretary.

Instead of delegating this visitor rationing to their secretaries two of the chief executives did it themselves. When the secretaries announced the name of a visitor whose business was not known to the executive, the latter went out and met the visitor in the secretary's room. Thus he did not need to ask the visitor to sit down before he learned the reason for the visit, and he found it much easier to keep the conversation short. For a similar reason two or three of the executives preferred to visit some of their immediate subordinates in their rooms instead of having them come in to the chief executive's office.

One of the executives studied tried to use fixed visiting hours during the week for those subordinates whom he had to see regularly. By this arrangement a certain pressure was put on the subordinates in question to take decisions by themselves. Having to save up their questions for the weekly conversation with the chief executive they were able to prepare them and to group them together much better than before. This system had been in force only a short time when we made the study, but it seemed to be working out well.

With respect to their use of telephone considerable personal differences existed between the different executives. Some of them answered all incoming calls from the outside directly, while others let their private secretaries or the telephone exchange operators find out the names of the persons calling and the reasons for their calls first before answering. The differences in these respects were due mainly to the character of business and to personal habits. As a whole, however, the rules regarding telephone calls were much more restrictive than those regarding personal visitors. Nevertheless the interruptions caused by telephone calls were one of the main causes of irritation for several of the chief executives. But Sweden has the largest number of telephones in Europe relatively to the population, and these telephones are used very extensively.

Although our recording of the executives' internal telephone calls was rather incomplete, it was our impression that these calls were much less of a problem than the telephone contacts with the outside. The way in which the telephone is used inside the firms is determined to a large extent by tradition, and is definitely a status symbol in most organizations. Most subordinates would never dream of calling up the chief executive on the telephone, and others would do so only in order to ask for a personal appointment. In the firms where conference telephones were installed, they seemed to be used mainly for this purpose and for other matters where a quick answer could be given. When the chief executive himself called up some subordinate on the telephone the purpose was generally the same.

As Dimock has observed[1] telephone communication is especially suitable in two situations: first, when the executive needs information that cannot wait; second, where he wishes to follow up on a particular assignment or to modify or change a given instruction. It is indispensable for the chief executive in his contact work but is in no way a substitute for direct personal contacts.

---

[1] M. E. Dimock, *The Executive in Action,* New York, 1945, p. 158.

*Chapter 6*

# COMMUNICATION ANALYSIS

> Indeed, the invention and perfection of instruments for
> the more accurate and precise observation and recording
> of social phenomena must be regarded as among the
> most important developments in the social sciences. It is
> easy to point to the flaws in these instruments as it was
> easy to point to the flaws in the early microscopes and
> telescopes. But, without these beginnings and the patient
> centuries of undramatic labor, sciences like bacteriology
> could not have appeared at all.
>
> *George A. Lundberg*

## 1. VISITS BY SUBORDINATES

In connection with the description of the contact charts in the last chapter I mentioned that the analysis of these charts was perhaps the most interesting and important part of our whole study. This chapter will be devoted to an exemplification of this communication analysis, and as my example I shall choose the chief executives' contacts with their subordinates. The median figure for the time the chief executives spent in receiving visitors in their offices during what I have called a "normal working day"[1] was nearly 3 1/2 hours, and the range varied from 1 3/4 hours to 5 hours. Conferences and private talks with visitors in the office were also the most time-consuming of the various occupations recorded for all but three of the executives, and most of these visitors were subordinates.

There are three different aspects of the subordinates' visits that will be discussed:

---

[1] Cf. p. 63.

their frequency and duration;
the nature of the questions dealt with; and
the kind of action they gave rise to.

As before the discussion will be centred around a hypothetical case, but this is of little importance since the main purpose is to exemplify the diagnosing technique.

## 2. FREQUENCY AND DURATION OF VISITS

Although one must be very cautious in drawing any conclusions from a mere study of a contact chart, such a study is of great help for the detection of the contact problems that require to be investigated. If we return to the contact chart illustrated in figure 10, we may e. g. ask ourselves

why the managing director in question has seen the Works Manager at "Factory B" 15 times, 8 of which times he saw him alone, while he has seen the Works Manager at "Factory A" only 5 times;

why he has had contact with 10 section and department heads in the Manufacturing division, but with only one in the Swedish Sales division or none in the Export Sales division; or

why he has had so many meetings with the Advertising Manager and the artist working in the Advertising section.

A further study may show that the answer on questions like these may be merely the seasonal character of the business, or the chance appearance of some problem that the chief executive is having to concentrate on just when the study is being made. But it may also disclose real weaknesses in the communication system. As a consequence of the increasing time the chief executive has to spend on outside activities, his contacts with certain divisions or personnel groups inside the firm may have diminished or been entirely broken off without his desiring or even noticing it. The *entré* to his office may have become more and more the preserve of the aggressive among his subordinates, or of those subordinates who have their offices close to his own. The chief executives' personal interests and preferences may also influence the communication patterns, personal likes and dislikes etc. After all, chief executives are only human.

"Physical propinquity may be a very real factor in determining the frequency of real communication," writes Simon, "and hence, the layout of officies is one of the important formal determinants of the communication system."[1] This observation was verified all through our study. It was most obvious, of course, in the case of those firms which had works or offices in different localities, but it was also true with regard to the home plant or the head office. A different part of the building or even different floor from that where the chief executive's office was situated meant in most cases a definite contact barrier. Two of the chief executives had consciously planned the lay-out of their head offices with consideration to the kind of communications they wanted, and they had succeeded in doing so. One of them had moved two divisional heads to another floor, because he wanted them to work more independently, and had placed two others near his own office, because he needed to be in close contact with them for his own work.

The contact charts were found to be especially valuable for the detection of short-cuts and short-circuits in the communication lines. Direct communication between the chief executive and a subordinate on the sectional or departmental level without the presence of their superior is, of course, something that happens and must happen every day in an organization. But when these contacts become too frequent

[1] H. A. Simon, *Administrative Behaviour, op. cit.* p. 158.

and when they diverge too much from the formal lines of communication, it is often a sign of some administrative weakness or maladjustment.

If for example, as in fig. 10, the managing director has had 8 private talks with the Works Manager in Factory B, but only 4 with his superior, or only one with the Works Manager in Factory A, these contacts may be purely chance phenomena or they may be the logical consequence of the present organizational structure of the manufacturing division. In our study we found similar cases of frequent contacts between the chief executive and sectional heads which could be explained merely by the fact that the divisional head in question had so many outside engagements that he could not be available to his subordinates when they wanted to consult him. But such short-cuts may also be a sign of an unconscious or conscious by-passing of a divisional head. In most cases the managing directors themselves are not aware of such matters, but these things are so much the more observed by their subordinates, and the amount of frustration and hard feelings they can give rise to is remarkable.

### 3.   NATURE OF QUESTIONS HANDLED

As was described in Chapter 2[1] we asked the chief executives to inform us what questions they actually dealt with during their contacts with subordinates and other visitors. We supplied them with a standardized questionnaire containing headings regarding three different aspects of the questions handled:

a. the fields of activity
b. questions of development and of current operations, and
c. questions of policy and of application,

---

[1] Cf. pp. 45 ff.

and the executives were asked to tick the appropriate headings for every question that came up. But, as I said before, we generally received only one questionnaire filled in for every visitor, even where more than one subject had been discussed during one and the same visit. The headings relating to (b) questions of development and of current operations, and to (c) questions of policy and of application were exactly the same on all questionnaires. Although we tried to do our best to explain to the individual executives what we meant by these terms it had to be left to them to interpret the meaning of these concepts in connection with the special items brought up for discussion.

The headings regarding (a) the fields of activity, on the other hand, were made up in cooperation with each individual executive and consequently varied to some extent from one case to another. Some headings such as "finance", "accountancy", "personnel" and "sales" were used in all studies, but in one case "sales" could be divided into two sub-classes and in another "personnel" included also "public relations". Other headings like "cost control", "research" and "technical development" were used by some executives but not by others. With the kind of data we thus had at our disposal, it was of course difficult to make any comparisons as between the different chief executives regarding the kind of questions handled, and we had to be on our guard against this difficulty the few times such comparisons were made.

These data regarding the questions discussed during the chief executives' meetings with their subordinates were presented graphically in diagrams of the type shown in figure 11 (facing p. 104). The number of headings for fields of activity shown in this diagram has been limited to 8 in order to save space, while in the actual studies the corresponding number varied from 9 to 13. (In most other respects fig. 11 resembles the diagrams actually produced.)

These charts on question classification should be seen in connection with the contact charts earlier discussed. While the contact charts indicate the frequency and duration of the subordinates' visits, the present charts describe the questions that were discussed during these visits. Thus from fig. 11, we can see for example that of the 15 personal contacts between the chief executive and the comptroller, indicated in fig. 10, seven were related wholly, and two partially, to questions of "finance, accountancy and legal matters", three partially to questions of "buying" etc. During three visits development problems were discussed, and during 12 visits, problems of current operations; during four visits policy questions and during 11 visits questions of application. Of the 15 contacts between the chief executive and the comptroller, these two met in a two-man discussion only once and on that occasion they discussed a policy question in the field of "finance", which was also classified as current operations.

While the right hand side of the diagram shows how the contacts with every *subordinate* are distributed with respect to questions of development or current operations, and policy or application, a similar distribution is given at the bottom of the diagram for all questions related to the same *field of activity*. Thus, of 13 questions related to "finance, accountancy and legal matters", two were classified as development questions and 11 as questions of current operations, while three were regarded as questions of policy and 10 as questions of application.

The type of question-classification chart here shown, indicates only the frequency of the various types of questions. The time the chief executive spent on these questions could, however, also be calculated, since the primary data contained information about the duration of every visit. But for diagnostic purposes it was generally sufficient to analyse the frequency distribution of the various types of questions.

These question-classification charts were mainly used — like the contact charts — as a diagnostic tool for the detection of the problems which should be investigated further. As such they were of great help. A study of a diagram like that illustrated in fig. 11 automatically gives rise to a large number of questions. One may ask, for example,

> why production questions have been discussed so much more often than questions of organization and planning,
>
> why the chief executive generally discussed production questions with several people, but questions of public relations with only one person at a time,
>
> why he discussed questions of finance and accountancy mainly with people from that division but questions of buying with almost everybody in the organization, or
>
> why the majority of the sales questions were of policy type while the financial questions were questions of application.

As is generally the case in the analysis of management problems, it is often more difficult to formulate the relevant questions in a communication analysis than to answer the questions, when they have once been stated. Any research tool which can be of help in this respect should therefore be of value.

In spite of the difficulties mentioned earlier, in making comparisons between the different executives and in spite of the limitation in the statistical material, our analysis of the questions handled brought out some findings which were of general interest. One of the objects of this analysis was the attempt to get some ideas about the extent to which the chief executives had to deal with "functional" questions as compared with questions of a company-wide nature.[1] For this purpose we introduced the terms single-field and multi-field questions, meaning thereby those questions which the executive marked as related to only one or to more than one field of activity respectively.

If we assumed the relative frequency of multi-field questions to be an indicator of the chief executive's handling of company-wide affairs, our studies showed that this task generally was of minor importance. There was no case where the multi-field questions amounted to more than one-fourth of the questions handled, and in the majority of cases it was less than one-sixth. Even these figures are probably too large, since in many cases the marking of a multi-field question did not actually refer to one question related to several fields of activities, but to several single-field questions that were discussed at one and the same visit. But there are, of course, many questions which are of a company-wide nature, although they are classified as single-field questions. As will be shown below, many problems in the field of "personnel" and "public relations" belong, for example, to this category.

Although the marking practice varied somewhat between the different executives, they seemed to associate the multi-field questions much more with such fields of activity as "personnel" and "public relations" than with fields like "finance and accountancy", "sales" or "production".[2] That such would be the case was, of course, expected. Questions of personnel and public relations are not "functional" in the same sense as questions of accountancy or sales, they are rather special aspects of all the activities going on in an organization. A production problem or a sales problem may also be a problem of personnel or public relations. There may very well be divisional or sectional

---

[1] Cf. p. 48 above.
[2] The diagram in fig. 11 is not representative in this respect.

heads who will never have to deal with questions of account-ancy or manufacturing, since these activities can be placed under the centralized leadership of functional specialists, but there can never be a superior of any kind in an organization who does not have to take care of some questions of person-nel or public relations.

This special character of the personnel questions was brought out also in another way. While the chief executives generally discussed questions of "finance and accountancy", "sales" or "manufacturing" with subordinates outside the corresponding divisions only when someone from the divi-sion in question was present, this was not true with regard to questions of personnel. The following examples may suffice to illustrate this point:

| Fields of activity | Number of cases discussed with subordinates during the investigation period | |
| --- | --- | --- |
| | total | in the presence of people from the corresponding division |
| *Executive A:* | | |
| "Finance and accountancy" | 28 | 26 |
| "Personnel" | 13 | 4 |
| *Executive B:* | | |
| "Finance and accountancy" | 26 | 19 |
| "Sales" | 32 | 22 |
| "Personnel" | 19 | 5 |

Since none of the firms had special divisions devoted to "public relations", the corresponding data could not be obtained for the questions related to that field of activity.

Returning to the problem of "company-wide" as compar-ed with "functional" questions, it may be noticed that there was no statistically significant co-variation as between visits at which single-field or multi-field questions were discussed and visits attended by one or several subordinates. As regards their character of development or current operations questions, and questions of policy or of application respectively, the single-field or multi-field questions might belong to any of these categories. For one executive there was no definite tendency to be found, for another there was a clear co-variation in one direction, and for a third in the opposite direction. On *a priori* grounds the one would be just as easy to explain as the other.

Just as there were questions related to some fields of activity that were generally of a multi-field type, there were some questions more often brought up with several persons present than others. But here the patterns varied a great deal as between the different executives. With one chief executive questions of "finance" were most often discussed with several people at a time, with another questions of "sales" or "technical" questions. In one firm questions of development or of policy were discussed at the meetings with several people; in another, questions of current operations or of application. In order to explain these differences we had to consider the seasonal character of the questions, the organizational structure of the particular firm, the personal qualifications of the various subordinates etc. As one would expect, however, these conferences with several subordinates at a time covered people from different divisions in the vast majority of cases. These conferences were one of the chief executives' means for inter-divisional co-ordination.

As a complement to the contact charts the diagrams on question classification were of great help in diagnosing short-circuits in the communication lines. Just as the by-passing of a divisional or sectional head could be traced on the contact chart, the by-passing of a division in the handling of certain problems gave rise to characteristic patterns on the question-classification chart.

As I mentioned above there are questions in some fields

of activity, like "personnel", that are discussed with a greater variety of people than other questions. Nevertheless, the type and frequency of these discussions were quite different when the personnel division had a clear policy, when it was well managed and when it was definitely recognized by the operating divisions, than when the opposite was the case. The same was true for other divisions. Although the amount of evidence is limited one may describe the patterns associated with strong and able leadership of a division, as they showed up on the question-classification charts, as follows:

relatively few questions classified by the chief executive as related exclusively to that field of activity;

questions concerning that field alone being decided upon by the division head himself;

the majority of the questions brought up being questions of development and questions of policy;

relatively few instances when questions in that field of activity were discussed without the presence of someone from the division; and

fewness of occasions when subordinates from the division took part in the discussion without the presence of the division head.

Thus, we found the question-classification chart valuable for diagnosing administrative weaknesses with respect not only to the work of the chief executive himself, but also to the work of his subordinates.

In this connection it may be appropriate to point to an administrative weakness found in some of the firms studied. Not always did the firms have a fixed clearance procedure as between the various divisions for the questions that should be brought up before the chief executive. The head of an operating division might in some cases take up a question of "finance", "personnel" or "building" without having first consulted the proper specialists. To what extent

FIGURE 11. Question-classification chart.

A black figure indicates that the question has been discussed at a meeting when the subordinate has been alone with the chief executive, a shaded figure that the subordinate in question has been accompanied by someone else. A square indicates that the question has been classified under only one subheading, and a triangle that it has been classified under several subheadings.

this actually happened and what it meant quantitatively in additional work for the chief executives we never found out.

In one of the last studies made we considered for a moment including some questions regarding this problem in the questionnaire, but we decided not to do so. What we aimed at was a question like:"Was the issue properly prepared beforehand?", but the chief executive in question did not think that a question of that type would give much. This is, however, a problem that deserves further study. The evidence from one of the firms we studied indicated clearly that one efficient device for saving the time of the chief executive is to introduce definite rules regarding the preparation of the questions brought up to him. The executive, writes Dimock, "must educate his department heads in the necessity for clearance, and make them realize that it is not a reflection on their ability nor on the confidence he places in them. He must make them see that clearance is essential because every program involves some kind of work that impinges on that of other divisions. In most organizations, many decisions cut across the fields of two or more subdivisions of the enterprise. If mistakes are to be avoided, then all aspects of a proposal must be scrutinized by those who know what to look for. There is no substitute for collaboration. Administration is the co-ordination of the work of specialists."[1]

Finally there are a few comments to be made regarding questions of development and questions of policy. In view of the nature of the underlying data these comments will be of a still more hypothetical nature than the rest of our findings. What one executive regards as a question of development, another may find to be a question of current operations, and there may even be inconsistencies in the markings of the individual chief executive during different

[1] M. E. Dimock, *The Executive in Action, op. cit.* p. 189.

periods, between different subordinates or different fields of activities. According to their own testimony, however, the executives did not find it difficult to classify the items discussed with respect to their development or current operations aspect. It was much harder to determine whether a question were of a policy character or not.

In the majority of cases the questions classified as development represented only a small part of the total. It is therefore not unnatural that, when asked what particular part of their duties the executives themselves regarded as neglected, they almost without exception answered the long-range planning of their business. The increasing amount of outside activities and the difficulty in getting enough time undisturbed by visitors and telephone calls were the common excuse in this connection. It was noticeable, however, that the executives who were found to have the longest "work alone" time also were those who during their meetings with subordinates had the highest percentage of development questions.

The frequency of policy questions was even lower than the frequency of development questions. The reason for this may have been either that the firms' policies were already established on most points, or that there was a certain reluctance on the part of the chief executives to take up policy items for discussion. In order to learn more about this matter we considered for a while introducing a question in the questionnaire on wether or not there existed a definite company policy regarding the item in question, but this was not carried out. Our general impressions were, however, that there is a certain reluctance in the case of many chief executives to establish clear precedents or policies as guides for future actions. The reason may be that the organization in question has grown fast in size and complexity, and that the chief executive has never seen the implication of these changes for his administration methods. He is running a firm with 2 000 employees in the same way, as he did when it had 500.

The absence of clear policies may also be the result of a defensive position, which the chief executive feels that he must take towards the attacks made on his firm by politicians, trade union leaders, newspapers etc. It may also be the outcome of the feeling that too rigid policy decisions may hamper the necessary flexibility in the firm's activities. But even when the chief executive sees the necessity of policy decisions, he may postpone action because of lack of time. A policy decision is generally much more difficult and time-consuming to take than a decision regarding some matter of detail. But by doing so he becomes more and more caught in a vicious circle: he is too over-loaded by details to be able to take policy decisions, but the very reason why he is over-loaded by details is the absence in the organization of established policies.

## 4.  KIND OF ACTIONS

It has been earlier mentioned that our study of the kind of actions was not so successful as we had hoped. Both the concepts and the recording technique used lacked the necessary refinement.[1] Among other things we had intended to study the question of whether there were any differences between the various subordinates of a firm with respect to the kind of actions the chief executive took when they presented their problems before him. In diagnosing the administrative situation we should for example have liked to know whether some subordinates went to the chief executive in order to get their decisions confirmed or to get advice, while others went there merely in order to inform their superior about decisions which were already put into

---

[1] Cf. p. 49 above.

action. But the data we had were too incomplete and too limited in number to make possible an analysis of this kind.

As I have said before, our study of the kind of actions showed at least one thing quite clearly. The main problem for the chief executive in dealing with questions brought up is to keep himself informed. Of the various headings on our questionnaire "getting information" was used at least twice as often as any of the others. The next in order of frequency was "advising and explaining". As regards the headings "taking decisions" and "giving orders" there were considerable differences between the different executives. As might be expected the extent to which these latter headings were used showed a noticeable co-variation with the degree of centralization or decentralization within the firms. The following figures illustrate this:

| Kind of action | Centralized organization | | Decentralized organization | |
|---|---|---|---|---|
| | Number of cases | Per cent | Number of cases | Per cent |
| "Getting information" | 143 | 37,9 | 76 | 39,6 |
| "Advising and explaining" | 60 | 15,9 | 28 | 14,6 |
| "Taking decisions" | 55 | 14,6 | 12 | 6,3 |
| "Giving orders" | 52 | 13,8 | 13 | 6,8 |
| Total number | 377 | 100,0 | 192 | 100,0 |

One must remember, however, that the data on which this table is based were not particularly adapted to comparisons between different persons.

# Chapter 7

# CONCLUSIONS

Science moves, but slowly slowly,
creeping on from point to point.
*Lord Tennyson*

## 1.  DIAGNOSTIC PROCEDURE

Although the purpose of this study was never formulated in an exact way, there were, as I have said in Chapter 1, certain problems which we particularly hoped would be illuminated by our research. There was first the question of the managing directors' own working methods and working efficiency as such. There was the question of getting material which might be of value for the selection and training at the top-executive level, and there was the question of public relations and of how far the changes in the relationship between the individual firm and the community at large had influenced the chief executives' tasks. In order to learn something about all this we had first of all to devise and test a method for an operational description of what the managing directors actually did in their daily work.

To make an observational study of non-manual work is always difficult, and this is especially true of the work of managing directors in large firms. It is so varied and so hard to grasp. It is also different from many other kinds of intellectual work in that it is more a practical art than an applied science. To give an adequate description of an artistic activity is always difficult. "An applied science carries on its tasks by the application of ascertained princip-les to particular cases. Thus the mechanical engineer designs an engine for a special purpose, and proceeds to construct it in the confident expectation that it will do the work it is designed to do. Indefinable elements in the task there will be few or none, success will therefore depend chiefly on pure systematic knowledge and very little upon judgement, intuition, or personal skill. A practical art has no complete and sure foundation of ascertained principles. Its posses-sions are made up of separate and fragmentary conquests from the unknown. The items of its knowledge are there-fore incompletely definable and are preserved as the tradi-tionary rules of the art. Those are not *applied* like scientific principles to the particular cases, but are *interpreted* for its treatment in accordance with the judgment, intuition, and personal skill of the artist."[1] Like many other intellectual activities the work of chief executives is, at least in part, on the road to becoming an applied science; but this trans-formation has just started, and the administrative science is still at a rudimentary stage.

It is, of course, not only the administrative tasks of the chief executives that can be characterized in this way, for at the lower levels of an organization also administration is mainly a practical art. But the job of the chief executive differs from the job of subordinate executives in one im-portant respect. If a divisional or sectional head does not do what he is supposed to do, there is always a superior who can correct him. The chief executive, on the other hand, is himself for the most part the judge of his own perfor-mance, and if he fails to interpret the rules of his art or apply such scientific principles as there are, in the proper way, there is no one around to set him right. But self-observ-ation and self-correction is no easy task. As long as the work

---

[1] Wilfred Trotter, "Art and Science in Medicine", *The Collected Papers of Wilfred Trotter, F. R. S.,* Oxford 1941, p. 94.

of the chief executive is described in such vague terms, such as "planning for the future", "coordinating the activities of subordinates", or "representing the organization towards the outside world", how is the chief executive to know whether he is doing the right planning, coordination and representation? If, for example, he reads a standard handbook on how to run an organization, will not his reaction be: "But this is exactly what I am doing"? How can we help the chief executive in his task of self-observation? Only by developing a method which records his activities in observational terms. "If more 'practical' men are to make better records", says Lasswell, two requirements must be met. First, a question must be asked that seems to them worth answering. Second, a procedure must be available that does not interfere with their work."[1]

The diagnostic procedure used in this study fulfilled at least the latter requirement, and it was developed as a tool which was intended to be of help for the formulation of relevant questions. The recording of such matters as the time spent on outside activities or on inspection tours in plants and offices, the frequency distribution of "alone intervals", the contacts with persons and institutions, and the nature of questions discussed at these contacts, gave rise to many important problems that had to be investigated further, and it was a useful instrument for the detection of deficiencies in the chief executives' present methods of work.

In many cases this laborious recording showed only what "everyone already knew". Observational studies "do frequently show only what was generally *suspected,* but call attention to the *degree* to which the suspicion was correct and under what *conditions* the facts are as 'everyone knows'. The distinction is an important one, because social scientists

---

[1] Harold D. Lasswell, *op. cit.* p. 280.

frequently fail to distinguish between what they *know* (as science defines knowledge, *i. e.,* demonstrable fact) and what they 'know' as a matter of private conviction, belief and feeling."[1] The failure to make such a distinction is prevalent, unfortunately, even outside the social science circles. But it is quite a different thing for a chief executive to *feel* that he does not have enough time to work alone, or to discuss questions of development with his subordinates, and to *know* how much time he spent alone in his office during the last month, or how many times development questions actually were discussed during the same period. Also it is one thing to discuss in an impersonal and impartial way such questions as the possible by-passing of a sous-chef or a functional head, when this discussion can be based on the findings of a contact chart or a question classification chart, and quite another thing to discuss the same matter purely on hearsay evidence.

The diagnostic procedure here described is, however, far from perfect. It can be improved and simplified in many ways, and some suggestions for such improvments have already been made. They relate in particular to the registration of what we have called kinds of action.

## 2. THE NATURE OF THE RESULTS

The purpose of this study was not give advice as to what the managing directors should do. Our job was that of an investigator and not that of a doctor. The primary task of a doctor as a craftsman is to get his patient well, while our task was to observe our patient's behaviour and to find out why he behaved as he did. "The mind of the craftsman dwells on what he knows, and he delights to use and to display his knowledge. The investigator's mind dwells on the unknown and puzzling, and his eagerness is often

---

[1] George A. Lundberg, *Social Research,* 2nd. ed., New York 1942, p. 28.

towards displaying doubts and difficulties. The adoption of a laboratory diffidence by a practitioner would soon ruin his practice. The acceptance of the easy standard of conclusion found in practice would similarly end a research worker's usefulness."[1]

The eagerness in displaying doubts and difficulties which has been demonstrated in the preceding chapters, may have caused some irritation to readers with practical interests. The main results of our observational analysis are in the form more of questions than of propositions. But the formulation of relevant questions is in itself a useful task. It is necessary as a starting point, and in the analysis of administrative problems it is often more difficult to ask the proper questions than to answer them.

But the result of our study is not only a statement of problems for further investigation. We have also tried to interpret the executive behaviour which we have observed. For this interpretation we needed a norm with which the individual behaviours could be compared. Now, when we say "normal" we may mean one of two things. "Most of the confusion regarding the 'normal' in the social sciences", writes George Lundberg, "has arisen from the failure to recognize the purely statistical nature of the concept as it is used in science, and consequently the complete relativity of the 'normal' to a specified criterion, system, social segment, or culture. Most frequently, normal is defined (by implication) as that state of affairs which the writer in question considers desirable."[2] Unfortunately there is no body of knowledge of normality in the statistical sense available having relation to our present subject of study. After half a century of time-and-motion studies of manual

---

[1] Sir Thomas Lewis, "Observations on Research in Medicine: Its Position and Its Needs," *Research in Medicine and Other Addresses*, London 19  , p. 21.

[2] George A. Lundberg, *Foundations of Sociology*, New York 1939, p. 213.

jobs, certain statistical norms have been developed for some elementary work motions, but we do not know, for example, how much time a chief executive of an industrial firm of a certain size and character normally spends on inspection tours, or what percentage questions of policy represents of the total number of questions that are brought up for his consideration by his subordinates.

In the absence of this knowledge the only norm we could use in our analysis of a particular behaviour pattern was the criterion of efficiency. That is, we compared the observed performance with alternative ways of performing the same task, or we called attention to the non-existence of certain performances which were regarded as important by the chief executives themselves. Since our immediate practical interest generally was the saving of executive time, the most efficient behaviour meant in most instances that behaviour which resulted in the accomplishing of a certain task in the shortest possible time.

The mere ascertainment that a particular behaviour deviated from the given norm was, however, not enough. We had also to find out the reasons for such a deviation. A chief executive who is overworked, or who is overloaded by details, is not much helped by the information that all this is his own fault. If he does not understand the "pathological" process which has produced his present difficulties, and learn to notice the early symptoms of such a process, he may soon find himself in similar difficulties again. The study of what I should like to call *administrative pathology,* that is, the study of deviations from admittedly more efficient procedures, and the causes producing such deviations, is a subject which deserves considerable attention. Of the findings of the present study there is probably nothing which has more direct bearing on the problems of executive training than the observations we have made in this particular field.

## 3.  IMPLICATION FOR FURTHER RESEARCH

Scientific research is not only a way of acquiring knowledge for the student who does it, as I have said in the
preface of this book, it is also a most efficient means of
exposing a lack of knowledge. Throughout the present
study I have, above all, lacked a theoretical system in which
to arrange the observations I have made. Of course, we
may proceed with empirical studies in the field of administration and even reach generalizations of some sort without
the help of a consistent theory, but as Talcott Parsons has
said, the highest levels of scientific development "are not
reached without conceptualization on the level of what is
ordinarily called that of the theoretical system. The closer
social science approaches to realizing this possibility, the
more mature will it be considered as a science and the
greater the predictive power which it will command."[1]
As a first implication of the present study on further
research I would, therefore, place the desirability of developing a systematic theory of executive behaviour. With
such a theory at our disposal, it would become much easier
to arrange the necessary empirical research in its proper
place.

Applying Parsons' ideas on the foundation of general
sociological theory, a theory of executive behaviour should
be

1)  "structural-functional" in character, which would
make it suitable for the analysis of dynamic problems;

2)  formulated within the "action" frame of reference,
thus starting out from the individual playing the "role" of
executive; and

3)  framed in terms of genuinely operational concepts,

---

[1] Talcott Parsons, "The Position of Sociological Theory", *Essays in
Sociological Theory Pure and Applied,* Glencoe, Illinois 1949, p. 4.

which is a necessary condition for its empirical verification.[1]

There is no need for me to dwell any further on the necessity of stating the theory of executive behaviour in operational terms. The concepts to be used do not have to be the ones employed in this study, but they must be genuinely operational. The requirement that the theory should be "structural-functional" implies that the function of the executive should be seen in relation to the social structure in which he is acting. This structure includes both the organization of which he is the leader and the society of which this organization is a constituent part. By focussing the attention on executive "action", the theory must consider the main factors determining this action:

the actor's knowledge of the situation,
the goals towards which he is striving, and
the attitudes which he has towards both the goals and
    the situation as such.

But the executive actions and the factors determining them must be seen both from the point of view of the actor himself and of the functioning of the social system under consideration.

The development of a theory of executive action must, however, be based on systematic empirical research. At present we lack sufficient knowledge both of existing norms for executive behaviour and of in how far and why actual behaviour deviates from these norms. Whether we ever shall reach a state of knowledge when we can speak of normal behaviour and degrees of deviation in the statistical sense seems to me rather doubtful, but it is a goal worth striving at.

In our empirical studies we must investigate how particu-

---

[1] *Ibid*, p. 5.

lar behaviour patterns are related to the social structures in which they take place. With reference to the general social background, the present study is limited mainly to the industrial society of Sweden. Some significant features of this society have been outlined in Chapter 3, and in the Administrative Problems Study Group we are at present working, as I have mentioned, on a more extensive study of the relationship between the individual firm and society at large. While studying the work of the chief executives of "Au Printemps" in Paris I had the opportunity of observing executive behaviour in a different environment, and this experience indicates that comparative research on this point may be fruitful. As regards the relationship between executive behaviour and the organizational structure in which they directly take place, some observations have been made in this book with reference both to centralized and decentralized organizations, and to organizations located in large cities and in the province. But these are mere suggestions for further research.

In our study of executive actions we have seen these actions mainly in relation to the immediate goals which the executives were striving towards. But the view needs to be extended both with reference to the more general objectives that exist, and to the attitudes the executives have towards these objectives and towards the means for their attainment. The studies mentioned by Henry[1] give some indication of a possible line of approach for such a research.

Another limitation of the present study is that the point of view has mainly been that of the actor himself. As I have said above, executive behaviour must also be studied from the functioning of the social system of which it is a part. Speaking in Chapter 2 about kinds of action I observed that a conversation between a chief executive and a subordinate, which from the former's point of view merely

---

[1] See p. 31, above.

means the getting of information, may very well be regarded by the latter as decision taking or even as the receiving of orders. On the whole, it can be said that we shall only come to a full understanding of executive actions if we observe them in relation to the simultaneous actions of other people in the organization. An extension of the present study on these lines is perhaps the end most immediately desired by the author.

# INDEX

# HISTORY OF MANAGEMENT THOUGHT

*An Arno Press Collection*

Arnold, Horace Lucian. **The Complete Cost-Keeper.** 1901

Austin, Bertram and W. Francis Lloyd. **The Secret of High Wages.** 1926

Berriman, A. E., et al. **Industrial Administration.** 1920

Cadbury, Edward. **Experiments In Industrial Organization.** 1912

Carlson, Sune. **Executive Behaviour.** 1951

Carney, Edward M. et al. **The American Business Manual.** 1914

Casson, Herbert N. **Factory Efficiency.** 1917

Chandler, Alfred D., editor. **The Application of Modern Systematic Management.** 1979

Chandler, Alfred D., editor. **Management Thought in Great Britain.** 1979

Chandler, Alfred D., editor. **Managerial Innovation at General Motors.** 1979

Chandler, Alfred D., editor. **Pioneers in Modern Factory Management.** 1979

Chandler, Alfred D., editor. **Precursors of Modern Management.** 1979

Chandler, Alfred D., editor. **The Railroads.** 1979

Church, A. Hamilton. **The Proper Distribution Of Expense Burden.** 1908

Davis, Ralph Currier. **The Fundamentals Of Top Management.** 1951

Devinat, Paul. **Scientific Management In Europe.** 1927

Diemer, Hugo. **Factory Organization and Administration.** 1910 and 1935

Elbourne, Edward T. **Factory Administration and Accounts.** 1919

Elbourne, Edward T. **Fundamentals of Industrial Administration.** 1934

Emerson, Harrington. **Efficiency as a Basis for Operation and Wages.** 1909

Kirkman, Marshall M[onroe]. **Railway Revenue.** 1879

Kirkman, Marshall M[onroe]. **Railway Expenditures.** 1880

Laurence, Edward. **The Duty and Office of a Land Steward.** 1731

Lee, John. **Management.** 1921

Lee, John, editor. **Pitman's Dictionary of Industrial Administration.** 1928

McKinsey, James O. **Managerial Accounting.** 1924

Rowntree, B. Seebohm. **The Human Factor in Business.** 1921

Schell, Erwin Haskell. **The Technique of Executive Control.** 1924

Sheldon, Oliver. **The Philosophy of Management.** 1923

Tead, Ordway and Henry C. Metcalfe. **Personnel Administration.** 1926

Urwick, L[yndall]. **The Golden Book of Management.** 1956

Urwick, L[yndall]. **Management of Tomorrow.** 1933